Lead With Love

Adie McDermott
& 16 contributing authors from around the world.

The Rural Publishing Company

First published by The Rural Publishing Company 2025.

Copyright © Adie McDermott 2025

Print (Paperback): 978-1-923008-28-1
eBook: 978-1-923008-29-8

This work is copyright. Apart from any use permitted under the Copyright Act 1968, no part of this publication may be reproduced, stored in a retrieval system or transmitted in any form or by any means, electronic, mechanical, photocopying, recording or otherwise, without the prior written permission of Adie McDermott or The Rural Publishing Company.

Cover Design: The Rural Publishing Company
Typesetting & Design: The Rural Publishing Company

The Rural Publishing Company
Website: https://theruralpublishingcompany.com.au
Email: hello@theruralpublishingcompany.com.au

Contents

About the Authors   1

Introduction   19

AUTHENTICITY IS TRUE BEAUTY   27

1. Give the World the Best of You   29
2. Desperately Seeking Approval   33
3. Love Your Youness   45
4. Disability Doesn't Define You – You Define You   59

STRENGTH AND RESILIENCE   73

5. Wonder, Whale Song and a Wholehearted Life   75
6. From Shadows to Strength   83
7. Wild Seasons: Cycling through change   99
8. Who Says I Can't Draw?   109
9. Just for Today   119

TUNING INTO YOUR HEART AND SOUL   125

10. HeartWriting: Your heart always holds the answers   127
11. Farmer of The Heart   137
12. A Lost and Found   147
13. Journey to Your True Authentic Self   159

WORTHY AND WELL	171
14. Pain to Purpose	173
15. Life Is a Puzzle	191
MAKING THINGS RIGHT	203
16. Ho'oponopono – Making Things Right	205
17. Re-discovering Joy in Midlife	211
SHARING YOUR VOICE	219
18. The Fine Art of Being Seen	221
19. Speak to Heal	235
20. Sa Ta Na Ma: Powerless to Powerful	247
21. Miracles. Magnetism. Meaning.	259
Conclusion	269
Acknowledgements	273

About the Authors

Adie McDermott: A multi-disciplined creative entrepreneur and an internationally published expert in self-expression. Adie McDermott creates collaborative programs and spaces where people can express themselves, in a way that their true voices are seen and heard. Using unique combinations of storytelling, writing, art making, community connection and eastern and western healing modalities, her world-renowned programs, workshops and retreats include the Lead With Love visibility program, Authentic Presence, Whole and the Art of Self-Compassion.

Totally passionate about self-expression, connection, self-compassion and our individual voices and stories being expressed, so we are seen, heard and loved; empowering women and minority groups to express and share themselves; challenging the way we see ourselves and our world as well as the beliefs we carry around with us – Adie teaches through everything that she does that our beauty, our happiness, our power, our potential and the quality of our relationships all come from authentically expressing ourselves.

Adie's natural strengths – connection, creativity, empathy, questioning and deep-thinking, special-interest research and her 20+ year self-development journey, allow her to see and feel things that are invisible to most. Question what others believe cannot be changed, combine creativity with strategy, instantly create a bond with anyone she meets, see the beauty in things that others do not (e.g. themselves) and find connections in things that others do not see. This gives her the ability to expertly support others to gently heal what is standing in the way of their greatest self-expression, to create more impact, to be more of themselves or simply just experience more joy in life.

A life-long learner and adventurer and a deeply caring soul, Adie is also a compassionate single mum and carer to an amazingly beautiful, neurodivergent and transgender teen.

www.adiemcdermott.com

ABOUT THE AUTHORS

Charlotte Fraser is a nationally recognised facilitator in sound, movement and stillness who uses a creative, sound-based and energy focussed approach, to provide opportunities for overwhelmed individuals to rediscover freedom through a deeper awareness of their body, inner resources and energy.

Founder of White Swan Sound and Yoga, a kirtan leader of tear dropping and joyous chants, a 'life-changing' sound healer and a quirky, creative senior yoga teacher, her kaleidoscopic teaching style draws on her passionate life outlook and makes unique references to nature with imagery to help one arrive at a deep connection with self.

Often light-hearted and always big-hearted, Charlotte has shared sound and movement at festivals, corporate functions, retreats, conferences, yoga studios, graduations, funerals and weddings to thousands of people around the world. She also teaches yoga to more than 50 people every week and runs yoga, sound bath and chanting sessions at a Drug and Alcohol Rehab Centre where she supports clients in transitions from loss and chaos to restoration and strength.

Charlotte holds Master of Educational Studies (with research in Mindfulness), BA in Social Sciences, Grad Dip Education, Diploma in Integrative Sound Healing, Cert IV Training and Assessment, Diploma of Classical Yoga and Advanced Diploma in Meditation Teaching. www.whiteswansoundandyoga.com

Imogen Ingram facilitates WomanSpeak™ workshops for Canberra organisations delivering services to women in recovery from addiction and family and domestic violence. She also runs circles for women in small business, middle management, and public facing roles.

Women who work with Imogen as a circle leader and speaking coach feel safe in their own skin, empowered to speak with confidence, and lead with authentic presence. She works one to one offering Emotional Freedom Technique (tapping), and a unique vocal coaching approach to message development, that enables small-business clients to deliver training, course content, and speak up for their business in fresh ways.

Stemming from her own intentional, unwavering inner work, Imogen honours the full spectrum of human experience in others, embracing both their light and their shadows.

Imogen's leadership as an embodied practice of grace, trust, play and celebration is fed by connection in community, deep listening, and movement as medicine.

Imogen restores in nature, finds joy and beauty in following the rhythms of the seasons, and lives with her husband and young-adult daughters in Canberra. Her current growth edges include spoken word poetry and providing Menopause Doula services to midlife women.

imogeningram.com

ABOUT THE AUTHORS

Kia Miller is a renowned yoga teacher, spiritual guide, and founder of Radiant Body Yoga. With a background in both Hatha and Kundalini Yoga, Kia blends traditional and contemporary practices to support physical vitality, mental clarity, and spiritual growth. Her unique approach has garnered a global following, inspiring students to experience the transformative power of yoga and meditation.

Kia is the creator of the Radiant Body Yoga Academy, a comprehensive training program that certifies and supports thousands of yoga teachers and practitioners worldwide. Through this platform and its vibrant community, she empowers individuals to step into their full potential, embody the teachings, and thrive both on and off the mat.

With over 25 years of experience, Kia is celebrated for her warmth, authenticity, and depth of knowledge. She has been featured multiple times in Yoga Journal, headlines international yoga festivals, and has a library of over 500 yoga classes on GLO.com. Her classes and trainings are heart-centered and accessible, guiding students at all levels to cultivate resilience, inner strength, and radiant health.

She leads workshops, retreats, and advanced teacher trainings around the world, emphasising yoga's capacity to connect us to our true essence and live with greater freedom, joy, and grace. Kia's mission is to demystify ancient practices, making them relevant and practical for modern life.

www.kiamiller.com

Lida Johnson is the primary Health & Wellness coach at Head-to-Toe Coaching. Growing up in an alcoholic and abusive family she struggled with her own sugar addiction, compulsive overeating, and negative self-worth and low self-esteem. Through this journey, she developed compassion to understand that making health changes is hard, confusing, and often not maintainable.

Lida helps individuals who are struggling and worry about their health – whether it's weight, exercise, disease, stress, sleep, or general wellness – transition from fear, inconsistency, and negative habits to empowered thoughts and beliefs by utilising proven systems and techniques for positive daily behaviours (rather than relying on willpower) that enable them to achieve their goals, embrace a healthier lifestyle, and show up every day as the best version of themselves.

Lida helps empower each of her clients to transform their health by providing research-based education, support, and compassionate coaching. Through this integrative approach, sustainable lifestyle changes are achieved by her clients.

Lida is a Certified Nutritionist, Personal Trainer, Health Coach, and Pre-diabetes Lifestyle Coach. She offers complimentary conversations to discuss your health. All the information to join her Triple-E Newsletter or to book a conversation is on her website www.headtotoecoaching.com.

ABOUT THE AUTHORS

Lynn Hord is a messaging specialist, intuitive business coach and breast cancer survivor, who teaches that speaking from your heart is the fastest path to being seen, sought-after and successful in your business – and life.

Over 11 years in business she has helped hundreds of women globally to infuse their heart and soul into the message they bring to the world and their purpose-driven work.

Lynn's own deeper initiation into this path came from surviving breast cancer in 2019, which stripped away false identities and ideals and awakened in her a desire to live and lead with more authenticity, truth and joy.

Integrating her genuine heart into her life and business has given her the tools, vision, understanding and practical steps to help others make that shift to greater soul integration in their message and work, with more speed, ease, and fun.

She does this through group programmes, Be The Channel and Raise Your Voice, as well as her Elevate Mastermind and 1-2-1 private coaching.

www.lynnhord.com

For 64 years **Mara Chambers** held onto the belief that she could not draw. Exploring where this belief came from –*was it actually fear?* – Mara questioned how true the beliefs that were holding her back all these years were. Putting herself outside of her comfort zone and challenging herself mentally by embracing, exploring and questioning a passing comment of *'Art is all about maths.'*

Mara is an environmentalist interested in *Reduce Reuse Recycle and Repair*, helping communities seeking assistance with sewing skills and more recently with compost making skills. Someone who has always been interested in sewing, she often used discarded clothing or bed linen to make interesting practical art smocks, children's clothes or bags. Mara has also sewn kangaroo pouches for local wildlife shelters, made over 600 face masks during COVID and provided them to local groups and the general public, made condolence bags for Geelong ICU Hospital, and she is always happy to help locals with clothing repairs.

On her journey of experiencing different styles of art in the last 2 years, Mara is now keen to apply these environmental principles in her artwork, looking at ways to include salvaged items in her art. Discarded bicycle parts and unwanted CDs are pieces she is now adding to her artwork. Her art is often both unique and motivating as she constantly asks *'What else can I do?'*

ABOUT THE AUTHORS

Melinda Charlesworth is a Coach and Writer working from Central Victoria, Australia on the lands of the Dja Dja Wurrung. Melinda combines storytelling, the magic of mindful movement and evidence based coaching techniques with a wicked sense of humour to support women of all ages to navigate the path towards self-acceptance and authenticity.

Her business, Adapted Consulting, promises to help you Feel, Lead, Be Better. Accredited as a Gallup Strengths Coach, she's proud to share that her Top 5 Strengths are Learner, Intellection, Input, Relator and Individualisation. Melinda offers individual and group strengths coaching and walks with you while you come to love and flex your own unique talents. Her favourite part of the relationship is being there when you first see your profile in the image created just for you.

Known for her ability to capture personality on the page, Melinda writes about community, belonging and human doings. Her creative work is loved for its sensitive yet raw depiction of women and their inner lives. When she is not coaching and sharing stories (and even when she is, to be honest), Melinda is parent of three (one of each), master of two dogs, travelling buddy to Himself and lucky Flock Leader of many Flamingos who join her on the kind of hikes that prove women of a certain age can do anything when they put their minds to it.

feelleadbebetter.com.au

Nicole Cullinan is an experienced health practitioner who has worked with thousands of patients internationally using her compassionate, innovative and holistic approach combining functional medicine, homeopathy and nature as therapy. She is the creator of Wellness Place International, an online health platform that bridges the paradigm gap between energy medicine, lifestyle and nutrition science and conventional medicine to educate and empower health seekers with more options to reclaim their vitality.

She has authored the Wild Seasons book series which will take you on a plant safari spotting edible and medicinal wild plants and show you how to rewild your diet with seasonal plant based ingredients. These books are both informative and works of art in which she demonstrates how common weeds could actually be your superfoods and plant allies in health and wellness. Using the seasons as a metaphor, she inspires those in transition and adapting to change in their lives, to follow the rhythms of nature as a guide to their healing.

Nicole is also a self care advocate who inspires her followers to have mindful rituals in nature and to appreciate how plants connect us with our environment. She believes that the wisdom in plants as food, medicine and inspiration, is essential to support resilience and heal many of today's chronic illnesses and disease.

www.wellnessplaceint.com

ABOUT THE AUTHORS

Rose Mascaro is a writer, editor and teacher who is passionate about teaching others how to connect with their most authentic, heart-led words. She's the former editor of *Teen Breathe* magazine, Australia's leading mindfulness magazine for teens, and holds a master's degree in creative writing from UTS, Sydney. Rose has written two books and has co-authored multiple titles for big names such as Lisa Messenger and Allura Halliwell. Rose is also a yoga and meditation teacher with a decade of spirituality immersion behind her and a one year spirituality mentorship training with Ava Irani, founder of Functional Spirituality.

In a previous life, Rose spent over a decade as a secondary English educator in her hometown of Perth. Hearing the calls of her creative heart, she quit her job, travelled the world, studied yoga and meditation, and moved to Sydney to study her master's degree and become a writer and editor specialising in fiction, travel, spirituality and lifestyle. In 2020 Rose launched *HeartWriting*, where she teaches powerful, authentic writing from the heart using a combination of literature, meditation, spirituality, and creative psychology. Her workshops are a perfect blend of spiritual connection and practical writing technique. Get prepared to expand in all directions, with heart science and philosophy, ancient Ayurvedic principles of harmony and creativity, the art psychology of Carl Jung, the creativity-enhancing Theta brainwave, and the many benefits of embracing a healthy, sustainable creative life.

www.heartwriting.com.au

Suzie Forbes is a passionate advocate for maternal, child and adolescent health. She has been a paediatric occupational therapist for 30 years, working with toddlers through teens and their families in both the USA and Australia. Suzie is an empathic motherhood educator and coach, mental health care practitioner, award winning speaker, author, and the mama of two kind, brave and connected young adults. Suzie has been featured on local and international podcasts as a parenting expert.

Suzie is the Founder and CEO of *The Wonderful Society* with a vision of empowering our community of educated mothers to cultivate wonder, strengthen connections, foster curiosity, ignite courage, and enhance emotional wellbeing and energy so they can mother with intention, vulnerability and authenticity within a safe circle of caregiving women. She believes that together, mamas can change the world. Mamas that work with her, talk about the increase in their confidence and the 'Suzie effect' that has occurred in their families – Suzie is someone you want in your corner.

Suzie draws from her own personal lived experience raising her own wildlings, as well as significant training in occupational science, neuroscience, psychology and trauma-informed practices, and the privilege of extensive experience supporting thousands of families over her career in her heart-led, family-centred and science-based programs that help mamas step into their own strengths and values to embrace a wholehearted life and raise happier, healthier and more helpful humans.

@the.wonderfulsociety

ABOUT THE AUTHORS

Tracey Summerfield-Owers is a passionate advocate for self-discovery and personal growth. Through navigating life's challenges, such as early marriage, divorce, and unexpected caregiving, Tracey has learned the importance of reconnecting with one's inner light.

At 52, after years of feeling overwhelmed by the demands of family and career, she faced burnout and realised the necessity of prioritising her own needs. With a deep understanding of the struggle to balance multiple roles – mother, partner, employee, and caregiver – Tracey invites others to explore their paths of rediscovery.

In her story, A Lost and Found: Re-discovering Yourself and Reigniting Your Inner Sparkle, she shares her transformative journey of embracing creativity and self-care, inspiring readers to reignite their inner sparkle. Tracey believes it's never too late to reclaim your identity and radiate your true essence.

Join her on this journey of self-exploration and rediscover the joy of being unapologetically you.

Dr Vasambal Manikkam is a talented Mauritian-born and Australian-qualified trauma-informed Nutritional Food Science Expert, empathetic and intuitive Yoga Teacher and devoted Holistic Health Promotion Practitioner. Exhibiting a unique, rare and authentic set of cross-disciplinary skills with value-added expertise in complementary therapy, she compassionately helps people take control and ownership over their own overall wellbeing, while healing repressed emotional traumas.

With an island touch, her wealth of knowledge, insightful wisdom, meticulous research skills, creativity, passion and love, she diligently teaches people that the most powerful resources to heal lie within themselves, and impactfully assists them to tap into and unlock these potentials. An award-winning speaker who has been interviewed internationally as a nutrition expert, an animal and nature lover, humble, resilient, never-married, single lady, Vasam fully understands life hardships, and advocates for 8 important pillars of health.

Vasam endeavours to serve by running interactive, inclusive, non-judgemental and culturally-safe tailor-made individual consultations, group sessions and workshops to empower people worldwide to transform into their best version with emotional and mental strength. The outcomes are achieved through an integrative holistic approach via evidence-based adaptive healing modalities.

Facebook: @VMEmpowersYOU

ABOUT THE AUTHORS

A UK literacy Champion, **Alyce King** shares her deep love of the written word through her writing, tutoring and book clubs where she teaches, inspires and supports others to feel self-confidence no matter their circumstances or ability. Alyce self-published her first poetry collection 'Feelings' in 2024 and is currently writing her first novel.

Previously an equestrian coach and skilled rider, Alyce became an online English tutor and avid writer after a life-changing accident saw her become a permanent wheelchair user in 2022.

Through the grief, disappointment and loss she experienced, Alyce worked hard on her mental health and learnt how to develop a new self-confidence and reconnect to the community as a wheelchair user. She now shares her story widely with others who find themselves in a similar situation or with minimal light at the end of a tunnel.

A UK Literacy Champion who firmly believes reading is a lifelong skill everyone should have access to learn, her tutoring sessions are focused on enjoyment and using interests and conversation to develop skills.

Alyce loves watching her students build confidence and self-belief whether it's in reading, writing or day to day life after challenges of all scales.

When she is not writing or teaching, Alyce loves to read and escape into new worlds.

https://alycekingauthorgmail.weebly.com/

Cecile Vence is a dedicated mum, community leader, Victorian Multicultural Honour Roll inductee (2024) and seasoned trainer with over 15 years of experience. She empowers migrants to develop their communication skills, helping them find their voice and place in a new country.

Cecile's advocacy is deeply rooted in her own experiences of overcoming the challenges of starting anew in a different country. She focuses on helping individuals to regain employment confidence and build the necessary skills to thrive in their careers and communities.

As a trainer, Cecile has facilitated numerous impactful workshops and training sessions, marked by empathy, understanding, and a genuine desire to see others succeed. Her work has been featured in Wimmera Mailtimes, Horsham News, Weekly Advertiser, and SBS News for leading multicultural events.

Growing up in the Philippines, Cecile was showered with love and support from her parents and siblings, instilling in her a sense of gratitude for her upbringing. Her transition to Australia was inspired by her three children and supported by her spouse, trusted family friends, community members and employers who believed in her.

Cecile's journey is a testament to the power of resilience, empathy and unwavering dedication to helping others achieve their fullest potential.

https://cecilevence.my.canva.site/cecile-vence-embarking-on-the-journey-of-embracing-yourself

ABOUT THE AUTHORS

Kirsten Wojtowicz: An integrated wellness expert, biodynamic farmer and writer, passionate about the everyday beauty and interconnectedness of life, Kirsten Wojtowicz creates spaces where women have permission to rest, restore and find their true soul-essence.

Weaving wisdom from a degree in naturopathy, decades of biodynamic farming and yoga studies Kirsten embodies seasonal wisdom and deep trust in nature's teachings. Connecting others to their true essence through the magic of slowing down and implementing simple daily rituals to connect with their hearts true calling.

Offering grounded lifestyle education that cultivates sustainable and long-term change for clients, Kirsten organically creates community within her business Wayfinder Wellbeing.

Always seeking a deeper understanding of the connection between our internal and external environments as applied to health, Kirsten embodies a simplistic, natural lifestyle, an evolution of decades of health science based studies, the practical applications of working and witnessing the land, and now meditation and yoga, she now educates others via her writing, workshops and personal consultation.

Kirsten believes a well brewed chai and writing poetry are soul medicine. When she is not working or studying you will find her sitting on her verandah enjoying both.

@wayfinder_wellbeing

Peta-Ann Wood is the Founder of Elegant Rebel® and Indie Reader Approved author of, *'What happens when they don't grow back – the upside down view of life after a bilateral mastectomy'*.

She is also a breast cancer thriver, having a bilateral mastectomy in her mid-40s. Post mastectomy, Peta-Ann decided to elegantly rebel against society's version of normal and chose to 'stay-flat' – meaning no prosthesis or reconstruction. She chose to celebrate her youness. No boobs required.

A talented writer and award-winning communication specialist, Peta-Ann's desire to assist other elegantly rebellious souls flourish, stems from her many years practicing various complementary therapies, alongside a stellar career as a communication specialist. This included spending 20+ years with police and emergency services, where she developed and led many award-winning programs.

As an internationally recognised author and now Holistic Coach and Oracle Card author, it was through her writing that Peta-Ann reignited her passion for assisting others to rediscover their true self and realise the answers are always within them.

Sharing from a place of lived experience – whether her breast cancer odyssey or being late diagnosed neurodivergent or growing up always being 'too…' – Peta-Ann's programs, books and card decks assist other like-minded souls find their own voice.

www.elegantrebelponders.com

Introduction

'As we let own light shine, we unconsciously give other people permission to do the same.'

Nelson Mandela

The most beautiful, valuable and impactful thing you can be is yourself and yet I know I am not alone when I say, it is one of the hardest things to do in life. If you are anything like past me you probably never feel good enough, you think you need to fix or change yourself to fit in, you keep yourself hidden and you don't feel worthy or value yourself, what you are skilled at, or what you know. You may also (like me) have a large fear of (or sensitivity to) rejection that sees you either alone or in unhealthy relationships, and keeps your true self hidden as you are simultaneously desperately trying to hide and to please everyone around you.

This, I have learnt in my 20+ years of research into why it is so hard to be and express ourselves, is not even our fault. Many things stop us from feeling comfortable to be ourselves. We are conditioned from birth to please, fit in and do the 'right thing' and we are often told we are too much if we are ourselves or that we are stuck up or selfish if we feel good about ourselves or assert our own needs. Our basic need as humans for connection and belonging (to be a part of something, liked and to fit in) are also usually stronger than our need to be ourselves. That is of course until we reach midlife and have a desperate pull to live as ourselves.

When Brené Brown researched belonging and connection she found many unusual things. She found that people who felt worthy did not mind being seen as vulnerable and imperfect, and that actually being vulnerable, imperfect and expressing yourself as you are, opposed to always trying to look or come across as perfect, connects you more deeply to others than anything else. Different is beautiful! We are all so afraid of being different or looking imperfect but it is our imperfections that make us beautiful. They make us interesting, memorable, real and stand out in a good way if we have a business and it is our imperfections that connect us with others. This is very surprising (perhaps shocking) to most people and so, you might like to read this over again.

To move past serious self-loathing, perfectionism, shame etc. and move from co-dependency and hiding myself and my needs away to expressing myself, allowing myself to feel good about myself, connect and be seen and loved in my own life now, I have learned to look at things in a backward way ...

We are all born as love, a beautiful little being with no thoughts of not being good enough and unconditional love for everyone and everything around us. I truly believe that at our core we are all still beautiful, unique and divine beings. Therefore, it makes sense when I say that we have all had this wrong all along. We don't need to fix or change ourselves, or try harder to be enough, we are already enough, a masterpiece in fact, and we instead just need to undo the lies we have been told, change the stories in our heads, and peel back the layers to who we innately are.

What I am suggesting is not easy, but looking at yourself in this way is a very good starting point. There are many ways you can start to change your life, to peel back the layers, change your thoughts and beliefs about yourself and create a life you love, your way and you will find many ways to do this in this book.

Most of us blame others for how we feel about ourselves, and are stuck somewhere in the past as this blame is often directed at our parents or our upbringing. No matter what has happened we can't change our past, but we can change how we feel about it, how we react to things now, how we see, treat and express ourselves and start to learn how to move forward in kinder, more loving and more connected ways.

The thing that makes the biggest difference throughout life – our relationships, our success at work or in business, and even when we make art – is not skills, experience or even good looks. It is self-acceptance, self-compassion, how well and how much we allow ourselves to express ourselves as we truly are.

I always saw ego as a characteristic in someone who thought highly of themselves. Someone who liked or loved themselves, saw themselves as good looking, highly skilled, better than others etc. The more I have learnt about human behaviour and human connection, I see how ego (even more strongly) affects the actions of people that don't accept, like or value themselves.

If we weren't taught as a child (and most of us were not) to express ourselves freely, that it was ok to reveal our true self and be loved as we truly were, there is still a child in us that is hurt and looking to fill these needs now as an adult.

In fact, I would go as far to say we 'desperately' seek to get them met, and that every day most interactions with other people become about getting our needs met. Our core needs for love, acceptance, appreciation, validation, connection and for being held, seen and heard for who we truly are.

How do we do this? We try to perfect ourselves, control everything, to make the uncertain certain and be sooo super pleasing so we get the validation we still need from others.

Most women are masters of disguise. We silence our needs and opinions and put on an outward appearance of happiness, control and perfection to please other people and to pretend we feel ok, but … the truth is we are constantly comparing ourselves to others, feel really unhappy when others do not react or act in a way we would like or expect them to, and feel empty, lost and honestly exhausted constantly trying to be someone else's version of ourselves so we are loved.

If you are not used to expressing yourself authentically in life, it is going to be very hard (when you first try) to express yourself creatively. In-turn, even if you do not think of yourself as an artist, you can use an expressive art practice to learn to express yourself more throughout your whole life.

Perfection, certainty, control, expectations, comparison and validation are all enemies of creativity, true self-expression and really our happiness in life.

In life (as in an art practice) some signs that you are letting your ego take control and not allowing yourself to listen to your true authentic self are:

- Trying to make everything perfect, over planning, not starting things or taking risks as you are afraid to mess up.

- You are unable to let go of control, you need to know the answer before you begin something and always try to make the uncertain certain, instead of going with the flow.

- You judge yourself very harshly. You expect yourself to be skilled at things all the time and do not let yourself be a beginner at anything.

- You compare yourself to others. You constantly see them as better than you.

- You seek validation and approval from others. You silence your voice or your expression in order to be pleasing, not be too much, or to not bring attention to yourself.

There are hundreds of different techniques and tools to start to reverse feeling and behaving in these unhealthy ways and start shining your light out into the world, and this book is filled with ideas. Things like meditation and yoga, belief clearing, mindful walking, journaling and gratitude practices, looking for the 'wonder' in your life, using your voice to find your voice and trusting your soul nudges so you find and follow your joy, hear your long-lost self speak, live more authentically to you, start to take up more space and attract deeper connections by expressing who you really are.

As a creative entrepreneur and artist, using the gentle magic and medicine of an expressive, non-perfection based art practice is my favourite thing to use. You can use this whether you think you are an artist or creative, or not, as it is not about perfection, but expressing what your heart wants to express.

How do you begin?

- Grab yourself a cheaper art journal (the cheaper the better) and some art materials. My favourites are a black ball point pen, a basic watercolour palette, some acrylic paints, Posca paint pens, gel pens and coloured tissue paper and start playing on the page. You may not think you know what to do, but if you can get past your mind and your need to perfect everything and work from your heart, believe me – *you do.*

- Above all else, in this journal allow yourself to do the things that your mind whispers to you. This voice is the long lost YOU, trying to tell you what you love, how you can express yourself and how you would love to do things. Allow yourself to do this and get things wrong.

- Your creativity and self-expression are not used to being heard. Think of them as beautiful immature young children, your inner child that longs to be heard. Give this child a chance to explore, play, make a mess, learn and grow as she becomes able. Give her a chance to tell you what she needs and wants.

- Your inner child holds the key to the quality of your life as an adult. Give as much love to your inner child as possible by doing things that (by adult standards) seem childish – finger painting perhaps, colouring outside the lines, using your opposite hand or scribbling? This allows the child within you to start to heal and express themselves more.

INTRODUCTION

- Allow yourself to enjoy the process, as after all, it is the process that is the most enjoyable part, and the part that has the most benefits, not the end product.

- Allow yourself to be a beginner, be imperfect, make a mess. We are not judging you, only you are.

- Try to really enjoy and explore your materials, enjoy the colours, the marks they can make, the freedom, the play and the absolute joy of just putting stuff down on the paper.

- Try not to control everything and have everything mapped or planned out. Instead start to trust and become comfortable in the unknown. Trust the process, the fact that you actually need to get things wrong in order to learn and get things right and allow amazing unimaginable things to happen.

- Gently push yourself to start or try out new things before you are ready. This will give you the little amounts of confidence and trust you need to push yourself more.

- Work in a safe, private place like a journal that you can close and don't show your work to anyone unless you are ready to.

- And most importantly be kind to yourself. If you don't, then who will?

ENJOY this process and this book and always remember this quote from Steve Maraboli:

'Stop trying to 'fix' yourself; you're not broken! You are perfectly imperfect and powerful beyond measure.'

Lots of love Adie X

AUTHENTICITY IS TRUE BEAUTY

How can you give up people pleasing and start to be more yourself, as opposed to a version of you that you think you should be? Read on ...

Chapter One

Give the World the Best of You

Boundaries ensure we say yes to ourselves, so we give the world the best of us, not what is left of us after we neglect ourselves.

With creator of *Lead with Love* Adie McDermott.

Does your fear of not being enough, **of being judged, rejected or disliked stop you from being yourself and living a life you want? If you said yes to this, you are certainly not alone.**

Women especially suffer from perfectionism, a preconditioned, deep desire (you could call it an affliction) to please everyone, to do it all and to put everybody else's needs ahead of their own; without ever letting anyone see them suffer. They are well known to have a habit of saying yes to everybody that needs them, then having no time for themselves, to do things that bring them joy and light them up.

Giving all your time away to others is one of the most common blocks to creativity and as a recovering codependent and chronic people pleaser myself, I am intimately familiar with giving everything to others and disregarding myself and my own needs.

In the past my life has been paralysed by my own very strong self-doubts, self-loathing, perfectionism and my need to please others. I never felt it was ok to express myself and desperately tried to perfect and control everything to the point that there was no way I could enjoy my life. I put my needs to the side in every interaction I had, every day, in an attempt to please everyone and regain the self-worth and love I didn't have, and I was constantly being left drained, unhappy, unfulfilled with nothing left to give.

I felt like a beautiful butterfly stuck in a jar without the lid on. I could fly out, but something was not allowing me to, something was broken and I did not know how to fix it and find my wings to fly. In time I realised the 'something' that was broken was ME, that self-acceptance, self-compassion were the things that were missing, and that giving myself away every day to others, then having nothing left for myself was the thing that was not allowing me to fly.

In the past, self-care seemed selfish and doing things I loved all for myself didn't even cross my mind. After many incidents of hitting rock bottom, picking myself up only to have it happen again, I finally discovered saying yes to everyone else was actually saying no to me and my own self-care, and that it was up to me to do something about this.

Here's a few things I discovered: If you are not used to it, it takes extreme amounts of courage to say no to others and to give to yourself. Others cannot fill your emptiness void, only you can. When your personal feelings of security, self-confidence and self-worth are based on the approval of others, it makes you very unwilling to disappoint someone, or put yourself in a situation where you might make others angry, or hurt their feelings ... but it is possible to do this *and still be loved.*

Here's what I would like to share with you ... believe it or not, self-care *is not selfish*. If that means saying no to others and yes to yourself, then that is totally ok. You cannot give anything to anybody if you are so drained you have nothing left to give. You can only take care of the world, everyone you know and everyone you love when you take care of yourself first, therefore setting boundaries that uphold your own self-care is not only a self-compassionate act, but an act of love for everyone else around you.

Being compassionate and loving to others does not mean giving all your time away, being a pushover or a doormat. Saying no to things that are not ok with you does not make you cold-hearted or an unkind person.

According to Brené Brown, a leading researcher in this field, the opposite is true. And in fact she has been quoted to say that *'The most compassionate people I have ever interviewed over the last 13 years were also the most boundaried.'*

And that boundaries not only create respect and say 'this is not ok with me', they allow us to be our most generous, loving and empathetic to others. If you haven't yet, I highly recommend watching Brené's eye opening boundaries interview. You will find the link to it in the story references.

To be clear, I am not suggesting that doing things for others necessarily makes you codependent or a people pleaser like I was. Giving yourself away can happen to any giving, sensitive person. Highly sensitive, empathetic people are most at risk as they don't just feel compassion for others, they feel the feelings of others as if they were their own. Empathy and kindness inspires their actions and understanding and it is what drives their need to help out.

The problem is empathy without your own boundaries set in place leads to self-neglect.

There is a lot of evidence that unhappiness in life and even most forms of depression, anxiety and substance abuse come from having unmet needs, not a chemical imbalance, disease or a biological problem. And that you, yourself, can choose to do something about them.

I am also certainly not suggesting that you should give up doing things for others all together. That would be selfish. I am suggesting however that YOU are also worth doing things for, that you need to make time for yourself so you have more to give to others, set boundaries, and find a healthy balance between giving and receiving.

Just knowing all this is acceptable and that it is ok to ask yourself, *'What are my needs?' 'How much of my time, energy and resources do I need to meet them?' 'What do I genuinely want to do for others?' 'How much of my time do I want to give to helping others meet their needs?'* has really helped me and I hope it helps you too.

References

- https://www.youtube.com/watch?v=TLOoa8UGqxA

Chapter Two

Desperately Seeking Approval

The life-affirming power of seeing who you are and liking who you see.

> With Melinda Charlesworth, Accredited Gallup Strengths coach, mindful walking and hiking fanatic, and partner at Adapted Consulting, where she leads executives to Feel, Lead, Be Better.

According to Psychology Today: *'Women are more likely to be people-pleasers. Society raises us to seek approval from others to tell us if we're doing the 'right' thing. A people-pleasing woman will do anything to avoid conflict and make things easier for those around her. She considers labels like 'high-maintenance' or 'fussy' to be failures and she unconsciously contributes to the continuation of societal expectations by conforming'.*

The feminist movement made inroads in the 1960s and 70s, sure, gaining rights for women that were pipe dreams for our grandmothers. All it's done, though, is move the explicit teaching of 'how to be a good girl' from explicit to a behaviour modification upbringing we all unconsciously absorb.

That's why, in nearly every culture, we're the carers. The health workforce, of which I was a loyal member for nearly three decades, is predominantly staffed by women – over two-thirds globally (World Health Organisation) and in some roles like nursing, nearly 90%. Health professionals return day after day excusing abuse from patients by telling themselves *'They couldn't help it'* or *'it's the illness'*. They allow the hierarchy to pay them far less than they're worth because *'we're not doing it for reward, we're doing it because we care'*. We don't need thanks; we're just doing our job ...'

Breaking free of people pleasing is no easy feat but it can be done. I know this because I spent most of my life judging my worth by measuring myself against the feedback I received from others. I feared rejection so much that I did everything I could to receive that elusive praise. I compromised my values and ignored that inner voice until it very nearly gave up trying to get my attention. I was unheard and unappreciated at work; I was emotionally and spiritually exhausted and I felt imprisoned.

It took reaching the lowest point in my life to find my way out and the way out was on foot.

Mindful walking led me out of people pleasing and returned my inner spirit. So much more than exercise, walking quietened my mind so I could tune into what I was feeling and needing until I could name it. Eventually, walking led me to the very thing that allowed me to finally see and accept myself as I naturally am. It was a simple test that said everything. The results speak for themselves – I liked it so much that I made it my career.

Let me tell you more ...

A picture tells a thousand words

'Oh! That's it! That's me!'

He handed over an image generated using words that resonated with my talents. Uniquely, perfectly, me. I stared at it in wonder and, unexpectedly, with love. This is me, I thought, and *I'm beautiful.*

Self-acceptance is glorious when it's finally yours.

I'd always scoffed at words like 'authentic' and 'self-acceptance'. They were firmly in the camp of the alternative types. You know, the ones who the people I knew called 'a bit woo woo'. It was not cool to be 'a bit woo woo'. What's acceptable is to be clever, professional, and successful. I wanted to be liked and so I rejected these as unworthy of my attention.

Expectations aren't directions you must follow

We women are so sensitive to judgement. We choose costumes to fit the roles we play. They're crucial when we need to present ourselves at work, they're necessary for hiding the bits of us that we're not sure will be approved of by others. We pick up on what's considered desirable and fit ourselves into the costume that goes with the façade called 'the right one'. We might feel the rough bits but, after a while, we mould our insides to fit that costume. Generally speaking, like a 'one size fits all' tunic dress, it's not too bad. Not fantastic or sexy or flattering, it doesn't make you glow, but you look pretty good. Acceptable.

It's not so bad ... until the day comes when that outfit starts to shrink and chafe. If it doesn't happen before, it's highly likely you'll be feeling the pinch of it by those midlife milestone birthdays. You'll realise you don't want to suck your tummy in or expose that much leg. Perhaps you'll wish you could show a bit more? After such a long time shaping yourself into that façade ... do you even remember what your natural shape is?

A lifetime of looking into the mirror at a reflection created for the approval of others robs us of the ability to truly see ourselves for who we are. Even worse, it trains us to reject the gorgeous, natural features we were born with. It can feel hopeless. It can feel like it's too late.

I smoothed down my tailored tunic and pointed my love of words towards an acceptable career as a speech pathologist. Clinician first, then manager. Finally, coach. These titles sat very comfortably with me and ticked the boxes I had on the pathway to approval. Career. Secure income. House. Family. It's a reasonably forgiving type of outfit but can be a neat fit. I thought I was wearing that tunic of expectation with ease.

You may also recognise these characteristics (from Psychology Today) in yourself ... if you do please read on.

- You often undermine your own needs.

- You go with the flow that's dictated by others.

- You're generally very agreeable.

- You don't assert yourself.

- You rarely say no.

Facing my reality and coming up short

The story of how I was finally forced to look in the mirror is not, sadly, unique to me. Knowing that doesn't take away the sting even now, years later. Some lessons leave scars.

> *'If you don't have a seat at the table, you're probably on the menu.'*
>
> Elizabeth Warren

There are no rule followers quite like health professionals. Those in the boardroom were wearing clothes that can withstand the hot machine wash more likely to kill the virus. Black stretch pants and flat shoes were my concession to formality. Another pandemic edict was twelve people maximum around the table. All other chairs were removed. We were thirteen. My boss indicated I should take a chair behind them, technically in the meeting and I sat there, relegated to the outer, excluded from the board meeting. No-one even looked my way.

The shame of it enveloped me. Sitting in that corner I realised a huge truth. This insult to my pride and self-worth wasn't an isolated one, it was simply the last one. The visible culmination of all the small hurts and rejections in the one huge act of disrespect. It was the one that forced me to face what had been right in front of me.

Despite doing all the 'right' and 'pleasing' things it seemed that this role was completely and utterly wrong for me.

Walking away from what no longer served me

So, what do you do when that tunic is torn from you leaving you naked and exposed? First, you cry. I cried for weeks. I cried for my dignity. I cried for my pride. I cried at all the times I was bullied, overlooked and demeaned. I cried for loyalty and I cried for lost time.

Then I started walking. Hard and far and fast.

Walking is moving meditation

I had a lot to pound into the footpath. I walked through a sense of obscurity. I walked away from the career that was the marker of success. I walked out of financial security. It was the words. I'd spent my entire career silencing my own voice to enable others to speak. My grief for all those silenced words was overwhelming.

The powerful healing properties of walking have been used by spiritual and medicinal models for aeons. The dynamic nature of movement is a conduit to both physical AND mental balance; the simple act of moving divests the body of energy that distracts from (and derails) the pathway to inner calm. The process of lowering physical stress and energy while walking returns perspective. Writers, healers and thinkers the world over report employing a daily walk as a non-negotiable tool in their day. It's during a walk when the questions are answered, the plot twists uncurl, and the solutions become evident.

I needed all of that and so I kept walking. There's no shortcut to recovering from a life of pleasing others. As I walked, I realised I'd never been sitting at the right table and that really hurt. By the time I'd walked off the tears I was angry. I observed how easily I fell into agreeable behaviour. Habits honed over a lifetime were hard to change. I gradually began to recognise the markers and slow and then stop the automatic response. But I had no idea what authentic looked like for me.

And then, serendipitously, I walked towards the very thing that would be my gateway to understanding who I really am.

'Solvitur ambulando. It is solved by walking.'

Saint Augustine

Seeing who you are and liking who you see

The positive psychology based CliftonStrengths coaching model identifies natural preferences, or talents. These are the things that come easily to you, often so much so that you learn to downplay them. No talent is better than any other, every single one is potential begging to be flexed. Nearly 34 million people across the world have completed it and proven that your talents really are unique. The chances of sharing the same Top 5 talents in the same order as anyone else is a tiny 1 in 33 million.

For me, completing the assessment was an epiphany. I learned that the fact I adore words and language is a strength, not a nerdy habit to be minimised. My drive to constantly learn, my ease with collating information (and emails!), my innate ability to find a way to communicate with others ... These are talents!!! Obvious in retrospect, sure, I had only considered it from my long-held belief of what I 'should' be.

The little girl who hid from others to make up stories stood up and finally owned who she is with great pride.

Naming and claiming your talents

There is incredible power in knowing your talents. It's like being handed a wardrobe full of outfits made just for you, the perfect fit and style that sings your song. More than that, when you know your unique strengths you forever have a personal yardstick against which all future decisions, opinions and perspectives can be checked. I promise you; you will never be at the mercy of checking for approval from others ever again.

Can you imagine freedom like that?

As a strengths coach, I see professional women shy away from seeking out their talents because they think it 'should' be obvious. They're intelligent, high performing people in demanding roles. Uh-oh, shame and people-pleasing rears its head again. This is not about intelligence or education. This is about undoing lifelong habits – there's not a single person who finds that as easy as a walk in the park.

I walk alongside women everyday as they discover their talents and claim them as their own. I see their whole lives change as I guide them to recognise how these strengths make them uniquely beautiful and valuable. I create their images and, the most joyous part of my job, laugh with them when they let out that startled gasp of recognition and claim it with love. *'That's me. Oh my goodness, that's me!'*

Aim your talents

Woo woo, it turns out, is a term created to belittle a different way of seeing things in the world. Those words I'd dismissed, authenticity and vulnerability, they play an integral part in the process I know works. There is a way to honour the authentic in every person in every setting and the first step is doing this for yourself. When you're able to find that authentic core, you have the key to self-acceptance. We all want to feel better, be a little bit better, don't we?

It's a shaky path, that road to self-love, but I'm practising finding my own words. It still rocks me when I come up against disapproval or conflict but I've got my picture as my north star to remind me who I am. I threw out all my high heels and wear flats that are far from acceptable executive suite wear. I need to take care of my feet, you know. They're my most important self-care tool.

I now work with people who, just like I once did, are seeking the courage to finally see clearly in that mirror. Together we find the picture that tells their story. Can you imagine the image we'd create from your unique talents? I bet there's someone, something, in you, ready to finally flourish. Want to find out who you are? The first step is making your talents visible to you.

EXERCISE 1: Five Clues to YOUR Talents

Scan this link to get your free worksheet to reveal the Five Clues To YOUR Talents and join our community of women who not just know themselves, they love who they see.

EXERCISE 2: Try mindful walking for yourself

Walking is accessible in some form to nearly everyone. If you can propel yourself forward, you can benefit from the healing power of walking. Walk with a question you know you need answered and you'll find insights will unveil themselves to you.

What you need:

TIME. Not much. Even 10 minutes will make a measurable difference, ideally at least 20 minutes.

Footwear that makes walking easy. High heels will unbalance you.

Walking in nature is the most direct way to experience the power of walking, however you can experience the benefit anywhere. I've pounded the footpaths of my suburb, circling the same block countless times. I've carved a circuit through hospital wards and offices. Just move. While walking alone is powerful it can be confronting for some. Trust me and try it somewhere you feel safe. You can walk around your living room if you need to.

The non-negotiables are:

No digital devices. This is not the time to monitor texts or social media.

Set your intention before you set off. What do you want to think about? Nothing? Something? NAME IT.

What to do:

Start walking. Your pace is the right one. You're not trying to keep up with anyone.

Notice what you see. What's the path made of? How does the sky seem today? What people, animals, flowers are around you?

Notice what you can hear. Are their birds singing? Can you hear the highway noise? Is your breath loud, are your footsteps rhythmic?

Notice how you feel.

When you return to your chair, revisit each of these BEFORE you look at a screen or talk to anyone. What did you see? What did you hear? How did you feel?

When:

As often as you can.

When you need to work something out.

When you're feeling fine.

Share your mindful walks with me on Instagram if you like @adaptedconsulting and #feelleadbebetter

Chapter Three

Love Your Youness

How to seek your joy, hear your soul and elegantly take up space.

> With Peta-Ann Wood: Indie Reader approved author of *What Happens When They Don't Grow Back – The upside down view of life after a bilateral mastectomy*, soulful coach and founder of Elegant Rebel®.

I've known since birth that I didn't fit into the society-accepted version of normal.

You know, when you don't fit in because you're always too something? For me, it was too big, too tall, too smart, too emotional, too loud, feet too big, breasts way too big ... the list goes on.

With so many 'too' labels, throughout my childhood I was bullied incessantly for being different. I was the child who hung out with the adults and was very rarely invited to after school events. I chose to not focus on what others thought, as it was simply too hurtful.

For most of my life, my safe space was independence and self-reliance. I chose at an early age to not subscribe to other's opinion of normal. I chose to simply be me. A choice made for survival; it was an isolating choice. A choice that diminished my own self-worth. A choice that I discovered years later needed to be unravelled and re-defined.

As I got older, I immersed myself into a successful career. This became my safe space. A place where I could hide my aloneness with busyness. Because of my 'work persona' everyone thought I was a social butterfly – always working, no time to be social – not realising I actually lived in my own isolated bubble. I successfully navigated life using this approach – hiding to fit in, not wanting to be admonished for being too something, again. The ultimate act of masking and camouflage.

Does hiding or playing small sound familiar? For me, it was an actual life changing event which gifted me the space to realise I'd always been me, but I wasn't celebrating this choice.

Traumatic events change you. It's that simple. And this life altering event, led to a flurry of questioning my choices. Will I ever be viewed as normal? How did I allow myself to become so isolated? Why do we consistently ignore our intuition and gut feelings? Such ponderings have led me on a very interesting path.

Being the 'youest' version of yourself

Tell me, do you truly allow yourself to take up space and be your youest you? Your true self? Accepting your youness unapologetically? I was in my 40s when I discovered I truly wasn't.

I am living well now, but at 45 I was diagnosed with breast cancer where my initial surgical treatment included a bilateral mastectomy. This was my life altering event, as I have subsequently chosen to 'stay-flat', meaning no prosthesis, no reconstruction, and very concave ribs – or *divots*.

It was this one event when I discovered, although I was choosing me, I was hiding. And because of this one event, I also chose to no longer hide from other people's opinions. It took a few years, and many twists and turns, but I now choose to openly accept my differences, to be unique and elegantly take up space. To live the adage, *'not fitting in, is how I fit in,'* and be at one with this.

As you can imagine, freeing myself from the opinions of others, allowing myself to unmask and change my version of independence from survival to freedom, was not easy. There were, and still are, wobbles along the way. But I got there by using the tools in my *Elegant Rebel Toolkit* and a process I teach others: *Elegantly Take Up Space: Discover, Uncover, Trust, Flourish, Freedom.*

The main underlying tenets of this process is to love your youness, through seeking joy and hearing your soul nudges.

Discover your joy

It's rather ironic that a breast cancer diagnosis provided the courage I needed to seek joy, listen to my soul and love my youness. While this is my lived experience, I am positive you have an equally life changing moment too.

It was also around this time, I discovered how adept I had been, and am, at masking. I was allowing isolation and aloneness to replace joy.

Joy is where we want, and deserve, to live every day. It is not dependent on external circumstances; it comes from deep within our soul. It's a state of being. The busyness, brouhaha and drama cannot take our sense of joy – *unless we allow it*, of course.

The first thing I did in my joy seeking adventure, was quit social media. Is this something you've done, to catch your breath and not be surrounded by the opinion-din?

When I first unplugged, in 2015, I'd been active on social media for about eight years, and it had been instrumental in maintaining my mask of being outgoing and appearing *'normal'*.

By unplugging, I was choosing to do something different. I intentionally chose not to post or doom scroll. I also chose to go through my various friends lists and ask a simple question, *'Do you bring joy into my life?'* The yes responses remained on my friend's list; the others were cut.

This small action was the beginning of me intentionally seeking joy every day. Subsequently, no activity for a few months morphed into about five years of diminished activity. The consequences of unplugging were vast and often eye opening. To this day I still use the joy meter when I clean out of my lists.

It was through this process, I also discovered I had lost my true sense of community.

By unplugging I was able to start rebuilding a sacred community. I was able to determine where I wanted to spend my time – physically. Who did I feel most at home with or seen and heard? What gave me a sense of being uplifted and peaceful, as opposed to feeling invisible and 'too' something?

For me, it was hanging out with treasured friends, solving the world's issues in cafés near the ocean or chatting randomly to folks on my morning walks or enjoying the company of other breast cancer thrivers at my exercise physiology-led training sessions. Simple. Elegant. Joyous.

By taking these small actions, I subconsciously rebuilt my true independence. I remain independent and self-reliant, however, no longer at the expense of feeling isolated and alone. I no longer use social media to hide. I am once again active on my socials, but now I share my me-ness, in a way which works for me, and with an almost non-existent fear of being perceived as 'too ...'. This fear has been replaced by a more graceful *'go on, I dare you ...'* attitude.

Early data in the 2023 Big JOY project study, being undertaken through The Greater Good Science Centre, University of California, confirms what I teach to others, that seeking and acknowledging joyous moments daily leads to:

- an increase in emotional well-being
- feelings of empowerment
- feeling of being on top of things
- feeling more contented in relationships
- better overall sleep quality.

So why wouldn't you allow yourself the space to do some self-enquiry and discover what actions to take to live your version of joy?

My action was simply unplugging. It doesn't have to be complex. It could be standing in the sun, allowing your mind to wander away from your challenges or doing a walking meditation or maybe strength training or sitting by the ocean, cuppa in hand.

Seeking your version of joy will also declutter your inner knowing. Vital for your next step.

Uncover your soul nudges

Throughout my breast cancer odyssey, other cancer related surgeries, and more recently being clinically verified as neurodivergent – age 54, the one thing I relied on most, was knowing how my soul nudges me. I cannot promise I always notice, and like many of us, I've had a few 'oh come on, seriously?' moments. But, irrespective of the occasional process glitches, I do know how to hear my soul. *Do you?*

It is one of my non-negotiables when discovering and remembering your uniqueness and allowing yourself to be you. Although simple in practice, it takes intention and 'rinsing and repeating' to hear and trust your soul. It also requires internal clutter clearing. Your soul has more energetic space and freedom to speak up and be heard, when there is less clutter.

Your soul also looks for the most direct route to share information. It can take various forms such as signs, symbols, synchronicities, a sense of knowing or even a song randomly playing – so pay attention.

Finding your way is the first step forward. My favourite ways, and the ones I teach, are using Oracle Cards and understanding which of your senses resonates most with your soul.

Working with Oracle Cards, or Tarot, is a tangible representation of your inner knowing. It is a physical extension of your soul. It is not information from some external mystical being. When you pull a card, it is your energy in that card and your soul shining through the imagery and words. I refer to cards as *'having a coach in your pocket 24/7'*.

My other favourite technique is understanding which of your senses illuminates your soul nudges. Senses in this way are referred to as Clairs, which is French for clear. You may have come across clairvoyance. Hollywood normally portrays this as a very intriguing character, sitting in a darkened room, hunched over a crystal ball. And while the crystal ball may be a useful tool – the Hollywood version is not reality.

Everyone has access to all the Clairs – and one or two may resonate more strongly. Out of the seven main ones, Claircognisance (clear knowing) and Clairaudience (clear hearing) are my top two. Here's the thing though, it takes intention and practice to sense your soul nudges saying, 'follow me, you truly have got this!'. Daily intention to practice your Clairs, to trust the nudges and overrule your thoughts dismissing them as imagination.

As part of my intention, at the beginning of my daily practice I always include the statement: *'I seek the courage, commitment, clarity and focus to accept and understand my inner knowing and take the actions illuminated by my soul.'* This sets me up for the next stage – Soul Writing.

EXERCISE: How to start hearing your soul nudges

Uncover the magic in your soul nudges by accessing the *Love Your Youness Starter Kit*, by scanning the QR code.

You'll have exclusive access to resources designed to discover how to hear your soul nudges clearly – the first step towards loving your youness.

Trust your soul nudges

Although I have been sensing my soul nudges for decades, I'm not the most trusting person. Trusting your nudges can be a tough gig. It requires a belief in the intangible and your ability to take the small, determined actions every day. This is the true meaning of empowerment for me.

One of my confidence-building tools is Soul Writing. It is a practical way to see your soul nudges unfolding. This tangibility builds confidence and trust.

Soul writing exercise:

Soul Writing is a simple activity. All you need is pen and paper, and then follow these steps.

Step 1 – Centre yourself. Simple box breathing is the most effective. Try it. Breathe in to the count of four, hold your breath for the count of four, then breath out to the count of four.

Step 2 – Ground yourself. Whatever works best for you. It could be as simple as standing barefoot on the earth or in the ocean. I personally use a White Light Soul Star clearing process.

Step 3 – Question time. Take a deep breath and on releasing it, in your mind's eye ask, 'What does my soul need me to know today?'. Focus on this question and repeat until you feel ready to write.

Step 4 – Just write! Focus on your question and just write. It's akin to a brain dump, minus the thinking. It's just you, your soul, a pen and paper. There are no right or wrong answers either. And no need to clock watch. Your soul will let you know when it's finished and time to uncover actions.

Step 5 – Take action! When you've finished writing, look for points which leap off the page. These are your actions. Remember, these actions may be for today, next week or next year. Find them, take note and follow.

Step 6 – Gratitude. Thank your soul for sharing with you and set the intention you will take small actions to move forward. This closing acknowledges and buoys your soul, and that you're taking notice.

When I first started Soul Writing it was about trusting my inner knowing and finding the actions I needed to live my joy and follow my dreams. I have discovered the unexpected consequence of Soul Writing is, your soul has the space to 'ditch the drama' and re-write the story you're consciously telling yourself.

In fact, your soul is writing your actual story – not the one we succumb to when we're always attempting to fit in and be something we're not. Your soul doesn't subscribe to the 'too something' thought process. Your soul accepts you, as is, and encourages you every day to do the same. Soul Writing makes this easier to recognise. It's up to you to live it, and I am living proof anyone can flourish by taking these easy steps to hear your soul.

Flourish in your freedom

It can be overwhelming when you spend time thinking about taking up space, feeling free and flourishing. However, developing a fuss-free, daily practice is the key to being the youest version of you, you can be.

The tools in my *Elegant Rebel Toolkit* are the mainstay of my daily practice – and a practice which takes as long as I have, to devote to it. I started off with 10 minutes a day while I was creating my new 'habit'. This grew to 15 minutes within a month and 30 minutes within two. The increases in time related to how much I valued my worth, as opposed to how much I thought needed fixing – as none of us require fixing. These days I take as much time as my soul needs to write.

My toolkit comes with all my favourite ways to elegantly rebel, tap into my soul and work out *'what next'*. To be me independently, without the sense of diminished worth I chose previously. Some of the tools I use are:

- Reiki daily to maintain my balance of mind, body and soul.

- Movement every day – either walking, dancing randomly or strength training.

- Using colour to assist me navigate feelings and emotions.

- Understanding what colours and clothing styles help me feel radiant – especially after choosing to stay flat.

- Seeking joy and 'glimmers' every day.

- Sensing my soul nudges through music, cards and a simple knowing.

- Soul Writing every day.

My daily practice is now simply my day – no over-thinking. I am worth the time and intention. It's how I stay in flow and navigate fallen branches on my path. It's how I keep believing to freely accept myself and others; freely follow my heart and soul nudges with discernment; freely take up space, follow my dreams and live life joyfully, my way, without the need for external validation.

As well as my toolkit, it was through my *Discover, Uncover, Trust, Flourish, Freedom* process, I gained clarity on my soul purpose, and made some tough decisions. For example:

- choosing to be me, without the mask of busyness and staunch self-reliant, independence

- choosing to be me without fear of being 'too …'

- choosing to undergo the clinical diagnostics for neurodivergence

- choosing to stay flat post bilateral mastectomy.

It has also elegantly led me to:

- various international mentors and uncovered my passion for soul coaching®.

- paths forward in my studies and developing my first oracle card deck.

- publishing my first book and sharing my experiences in the hope others will also ditch normal and celebrate their uniqueness.

- establish my own business, after being medically retired at 49 years old.

- let go of my isolation approach to independence and focus on truly living – asking for assistance where necessary, giving and receiving in equal measure, and requesting accommodations without fear of perception.

Like many others, I was able to achieve this, because the process is about not thinking or allowing your ego to take over. It's just stepping forward from your heart and soul. And this leads to true empowerment, freedom and allowing yourself to flourish in all your youness.

It is a never-ending story ...

Fear and wobbles will still make an appearance even when you follow this process. That's because we are human and allowing ourselves to take up space is not our natural way of being. Our first response is generally to hide or play it small, as this feels the safest path.

However, by choosing you and following these steps, you will want to stand tall, shine your light and elegantly take up space.

Always remember, do not diminish your presence based on others' judgment or opinions. You are a beacon for others, so be the youest you, you can be. Your very being encourages others to take up their own space too, creating a positive ripple effect of kindness, compassion and grace.

When you take up space, you step into your empowerment, you are accepting of yourself and others, and you want to share your elegantly rebellious soul with the world around you. So go ahead, seek your joy, hear your soul, elegantly claim your space and above all, **love your youness**!

References

- The Big JOY project
  https://greatergood.berkeley.edu/article/item/can_little_steps_lead_to_big_joy
  https://ggia.berkeley.edu/bigjoy

Chapter Four

Disability Doesn't Define You – You Define You

Re-discovering your self-value by recognising the impact you have on others.

With Alyce King, UK writer of poetry and fiction and literacy champion.

'Disability is a matter of perception. If you can do just one thing well, you're needed by someone.'

Martina Navratilova

A life changing accident in 2019, left me with temporary paralysis, a 'shaken brain' and Functional Neurological Disorder (FND). The paralysis dissipated to right side weakness, the shaken brain morphed into poor memory and the FND continued. I have had a number of relapses of FND, leaving me with no speech, paralysis from the waist down and I lost my memory completely – literally – I woke up and didn't know who my mum was, or my partner. I had to write everything down to communicate, but didn't know how to write numbers. I worked hard to get my speech back, but my memory never really recovered from that, despite the best efforts of my mum and partner.

I had horrific chronic pain, always. The medication I was on was increased and added to, just to help me get up in the morning. I had my own business, I felt I had to keep going – no choice but to try. Then in 2022, following a decline in health and an increase in acute pain, I had spinal surgery. I spent 7-8 weeks in rehab trying to relearn to walk, but didn't get very far. I could slide on the floor with socks on, but couldn't lift my legs. My chronic pain increased, and my fatigue was debilitating. This was not the person I was. I came home in a wheelchair, prognosis not clear. Within five days of being home, I was unable to stand.

I haven't stood since, and now, it's highly, highly unlikely I will walk again.

Prior to this, I was physically fit, a horse rider with my own equestrian coaching business sharing knowledge I had spent years training and passing exams for, I was competitive in British Dressage, I could drive, I could walk.

I am now a wheelchair user. I am unable to stand, I can no longer drive and I have a vision impairment.

Wheelchair life was dumped upon me, as it is many others, without a warning, without a care in the world. Yet it changes everything, from where you live, to the help you need, from your ability to go to the toilet, to getting in and out of a car.

If this resonates with you for any reason, I am so sorry to hear this, but I am here to tell you that my disability does not define me anymore. I hope to encourage you to learn to do the same.

Our fears of being valuable and loved

Maybe you understand when I say that for a long time, I didn't see my place in the world, and I started to believe that I was no longer valuable, or loved, or wanted in my social circles?

But a number of years down the line, I can now see that I am still important and valued, just differently to how I was previously. And I don't want sympathy or pity, I don't want to be treated any differently to anyone else. Disabled people or those with long term health conditions are human and important and have every right to be a part of society as those without a disability or health condition – you may be one of those people, either struggling or a loved one is struggling and you may care for them in any capacity.

My biggest fears were that I was letting people down, I'd lose everything I knew and the purpose of getting up each morning. I continually questioned what was the point?

I was bed bound for months and months on end, my mother's house was where I returned to from hospital but it was not accessible, meaning, I was also housebound. This was catastrophic to my mental health. For someone who had always been an outside person, to be stuck inside four walls for months and months, was hard. I had some very dark days and thoughts, not knowing how to get myself out of the huge, dark hole I'd been sucked into.

Our pride and dignity

Have you ever lay around day after day thinking ...

> *'None of this is okay,*
> *This is how I spend my day,*
> *Laying or sitting,*
> *Looking left, or right,*
> *Washing out of a bowl each night,*
> *Talking or listening to what is said,*
> *But always in my bed.'*

I have and that's why and when I wrote this poem.

Maybe you've had a time in your life when you were unable to have any privacy to any degree – at work, or at home, or in hospital, or in a family situation? It drags you down eventually, it's degrading, it's inhumane. You will want, crave, need your own space, time and privacy.

Over a number of months, it truly degraded me, and literally overnight, I decided I could no longer wash out of a bowl. I hated it. I didn't want to be the girl that didn't shower. I hated wash time with no privacy. I hated having a commode as a toilet by my bed in the sitting room, again, with no privacy. *I literally hated life.*

Those I loved? I was pushing them away, not asking for help when I needed it, because I was stubborn and I had an element of pride and dignity. I was 26 when I had my accident, I was 29 when I became a wheelchair user. But age doesn't change anything. You can be born disabled, or you can become disabled.

> *'17% of disabled people are born with their disabilities. 2% of the working-age population becomes disabled every year.'*
> University of St Andrew's, Scotland, UK

How do you become you again after something devastating and life-changing like this?

The question that changed it for me was: *'What do we need to do?'*

My partner and I started looking for somewhere to live. For anyone looking for accessible housing – you will know it is like fairy dust. For those not looking but say there isn't enough housing, that's true, but try looking for somewhere that is one level or ground floor, with a wet room, and you will see, there are even less options available.

Eventually, we moved into a ground floor apartment, with a shower and a garden. The shower wasn't really suitable, but I believed it was better than washing out of a bowl. After two years there, the compromise is now not enough, and we will be looking to find a bungalow, with a wetroom and garden ... again, these are fairy dust, and even if you find one, you can guarantee it's not affordable. I'm sure, if you are looking for somewhere to live, you are struggling too, no matter what you are looking for.

Living with my partner, and figuring my new way of life, while he was figuring his new partner out, created a challenge, but one that we now share with laughter – but it was hard. Hard on me, but also hard on him – I was no longer the girl he fell in love with, my personality had changed with vicious mood swings, always cautious, no risk taking and I felt numb to any kind of feelings.

Life was different. I could no longer work as a horse riding coach. What could I do? I had no idea. I couldn't drive. Independent only within my own home, but my days were mixed. With chronic fatigue comes no or low energy days, or days where brain fog wipes you out, or the days where the pain is so bad, bed is the only place you can be. How could I work around these? I didn't want to give up, I wanted to do something, but it needed to work for me and my health.

Find reasons to live

> *'My advice to other disabled people would be, concentrate on things your disability doesn't prevent you doing well, and don't regret the things it interferes with. Don't be disabled in spirit as well as physically.'*
>
> Stephen Hawking

Finding things that I could do that I loved really changed my life.

I studied a Teaching English as a Foreign Language qualification, which reignited my passion for words, and the English language, but it also opened the door for tutoring.

I began tutoring for free the refugees of the Ukraine war who had been displaced to England but speaking little English. As I was previously a coach, teaching the English language almost felt natural, I was still coaching I realised, just indoors and with no horses! Following this, I started tutoring via an international tutoring agency which helped me build experience of working with ages 6 years+ and all nationalities, finding different approaches and explanations. This gave me a reason to get dressed each morning, and to look presentable. Then I was asked by a friend of a friend if I could tutor their child. I said yes, I can help with reading and writing.

Soon I had children who were home-schooled, and in school, learning with me each week, working to improve and build confidence in their reading and writing. I also had three students working towards their end of school exams. This was pressure – I couldn't guarantee a pass, but I would work hard for them to pass. They worked incredibly hard, and they managed a pass and more. But my turning point? Their thank you emails. This was when I realised I had played a part in their life, in their success. Me. The girl who didn't feel she had anything to give now she was disabled.

What does this mean for you? You can do it; you can find something you enjoy and do a little of. Consider something creative, or what is your specialist knowledge, could you tutor that subject online? Could you consult for it? If you create, could you sell your work? In the UK we have Etsy, or eBay, or Vinted, or if you can, set up your own website shop, or could you write a blog on your subject?

What's important to note here is I don't work full time, I can't. I struggle with part time sometimes. I work as it suits me, I have my regular students, and as long as I can keep on top of teaching them, it's okay. Would I like to be earning more money, to contribute to the household earnings, and have a better lifestyle, yes of course – I don't know anyone who'd say no to that – but, I can't, I have tried, it makes me unwell. I constantly feel guilty about putting all the pressure on my partner. He has to go out to work, work long hours (he's a farmer) all to ensure we have enough money each month to pay the rent, our household bills and put food on the table each day. My advice here? Talk, share things, snippets about your day, and listen to your partner's. You may feel you have nothing to talk about, but find anecdotes, even if it's about that damn cat pooping in your garden.

The joy of community connection

I posted on my new town's community Facebook to ask if there was a book club. I didn't expect what would happen. I set up a book club. We meet monthly, we have a few books to choose from each month, then we meet to discuss them, our thoughts, feelings, ratings and the other books we have been reading and want to recommend. Our Facebook group has 30+ members, and our monthly meetings typically have 10-12 attendees.

To my surprise, as we approached the one year birthday of our book club, the other members suggested we have a birthday meal – we go somewhere and celebrate. I couldn't believe it, these ladies valued their book club enough to go out with the other members, most of whom had met at meetings only eleven times.

At this birthday meal, my realisation of what this book club meant came full circle. One of the member's made a speech, in it, thanking me for organising the club, with respect and encouragement, providing a safe place for opinions to be shared and friendships to develop. As I sat there with tears in my eyes, I couldn't believe it. I was appreciated. In response to the wonderful speech and applause, I was honest with the group saying how actually, it was this group who accepted me as I am, made me get out the house once a month to meet ladies from all walks of life, with all different roles in life, and create friendships and a scene of belonging when I was at my lowest. Only one of the ladies knew me from my previous life, and she is my best friend. Everyone else only knew me as I am today, and they still absolutely accepted and are grateful to me. I impact their lives in a positive way.

Belonging. What a feeling that is.

To feel happiness and whole again you need to feel you belong to something. It can be really scary at first. Even joining a group (rather than setting up a group), can be intimidating, but, in my experience, pop the organiser a message, explain you're anxious and it's your first time joining something like it. There are literally groups for every interest – both online/virtual and in person. If you're not sure, or Google isn't helping, ask on your local town social media. You may even be able to do an adapted sport, of which there are now so many adapted sports, from swimming, to horse riding, to tennis, to walking football. Here are some useful websites: everyybodymoves.org.uk and moveunitedsport.org.

Did belonging to my book club change the way I thought? Absolutely. I now know I have a positive impact on a number of ladies, and I have made friends as a disabled person – something I had hidden away from trying. But understand – when I first became a wheelchair user, when I had no confidence or self-worth, none of this would have been possible – I needed time to accept my new self, and learn who I am, what I liked to do, and the people I wanted around me. For me, to have people who only know me as I am now, has helped massively, as there are no comparisons, literally or metaphorically in my head. That's not to say I dumped everyone from my previous life, I didn't but most of them still don't know the full picture (if they read this they will!), but I still speak with a lot of them via message or email.

On low days, I still have a voice inside asking *'What's the point'*, or *'You're not good enough'*. But I now have evidence that I am enough, I am accepted, I am valued.

> **EXERCISE:** I Am Enough
>
> It is possible to change the way you feel about yourself using positive affirmations. This is what I recommend. Write down the following phrases, and pop them where you see them often. Mine are in my pencil case, on my laptop, in my food cupboard, in my handbag, in my purse, and in my knicker drawer (always makes me smile!). These will help you feel positive and powerful again.
>
> I am enough
> I am wanted
> I am valued
> I am supported
> I belong

This is a list of other things that got me through my dark days.

- Reflexology – the knowledge that my body is being levelled or reset from the inside out at each appointment makes me feel like I'm giving my body the best help I can.

- Aromatherapy – true relaxation, this is truly the only time my mind quietens and shuts off. My aromatherapist is the kindest, most lovely lady, who is a great listener.

- Talking therapy – I had tried this on and off for years, and it never helped – for me, revisiting the past, the accident, the traumas, absolutely did not help me move forward. It's true what they say; therapy won't work unless you have the right therapist. I found a fabulous lady who I now meet with virtually, via Zoom, and she allows the client (me) to lead the conversation, often slowing the pace and asking questions to help reflect deeper feelings or reasoning. This has been crucial to me learning to ask the 'I questions' (see below)

- Facials – I always struggled with self-care, I had no idea how, or how to do it without feeling guilty or selfish. Self-care is not selfish. For you to be at your best, you need to look after you. So, for me, having a rejuvenating facial every 4-6 weeks, is my self care.

- Reading – reading is my escape. I love reading as it allows you to travel to so many worlds, and perspectives. You will often pick up nuggets of knowledge or inspiration from books or characters too.

- Writing – who knew that inside me, there was a poet and a writer. I started writing my novel in 2023, and I am hoping to have it published in 2025. I also self-published my first poetry collection in 2024, which I would never have predicted. Want to write a novel or story or memoir? Just start. Put pen to paper and start, start at the end, the middle, the beginning, or plan your character, do anything, as long as you start. It's a long process so try to enjoy every step

- Online Courses – I signed up to do some writing courses. I have done one so far, in person, and a few more online.

When things feel out of control or stressful, 'I' Questions help you refocus.

In moments of stress, wonder, and doubt, these 'I' questions help you to slow down and take back your control.

'What do I want?'

'What do I need?'

'What do I think?'

'What do I feel?'

You may not have an answer for each question every time, and that's okay – but you will figure out what you can do to help yourself – at no charge, and in a way that no one else needs to know.

> **EXERCISE: 10 day self-confidence boost challenge**
>
> Discovering self-value, realising the impact I have on other women when I follow what I love and my natural strengths, skills and abilities has turned my life around, allowing me to feel an important part of the world again. I hope I encourage you to do the same.
>
> With a few simple tasks it is possible to start to regain your self-confidence as a person with a disability or not.

This QR code sends you to a place where you can try out my 10 day self-confidence boost challenge, that gently encourages you out of your comfort zone, question your reasoning and thoughts about yourself and find light on dark days.

STRENGTH AND RESILIENCE

Stories, strategies and processes for replacing fear, doubts, anxiety and depression with joy, wonder, creativity, courage and a wholehearted life.

Chapter Five

Wonder, Whale Song and a Wholehearted Life

Learning to live with fear by embracing wonder.

> With Suzie Forbes, internationally renowned paediatric occupational therapist, motherhood mentor, mama of two wildlings, and founder of *The Wonderful Society* – empowering mamas to embrace intentional, wholehearted living and raise happier, healthier, more helpful humans.

Wonder and whale song

As the toes of her fins hit the water, I could see the large shadow below, its broad, crescent shaped tail undulating in its distinct side to side rhythm. My heart skipped a beat as she lowered herself off the ladder into the pelagic water with ease and grace. My passionate daughter – first to dive in, just 16 years of age and exhilarated at this opportunity. On the back of the boat fully grown adults stood and watched in awe, wrestling with their inner fear. As her mama, I was breathless with it. The giant outline of the shark passed by. My gorgeous girl lifted her face, so that even through her mask, her brown eyes pierced mine, wide with wonder. She gave me a thumbs up. I exhaled, enchanted by her exhilaration and courage.

There were two tiger sharks in that water, plus a shiver of sandbar sharks circling below. The larger of the two tiger sharks, five metres in length and known to locals as Kalihi, is said to be a bit 'spicy' – the regal protector of her ocean, her dominance commanding respect. As the queen, she claimed the highest space in these waters: all the other sharks dipping below in reverence. That morning, as the sun rose over the island, my girl got to spend time in the wonder of Kalihi's court, hearing the swish of her gills as she breathed not more than two metres away, floating in the wonder of distant whale song.

Those things we most fear – like an ocean full of sharks – are often entwined with the miracle of wonder. The Oxford English Dictionary defines wonder as 'a feeling of amazement and admiration, caused by something beautiful, remarkable, or <u>unfamiliar</u>'. These can be short, transient moments – and if we are not paying attention, they can be easily missed. When we experience wonder we are usually leaning into something we have not seen, heard or felt before, or that feels so much bigger than us. Wonder helps us to be brave. To act, even when we're out of our depth.

Fear and trepidation

Have you ever felt so very out of your depth? Like the sharks are circling, and it's only a matter of time before you succumb?

Rewind ten years and this was me. My precious kids and I had survived trauma, and as anyone who has walked this path knows, we had not come out unscathed. My son was already a highly perceptive child – the world was too loud, too fast, too much for him, but now he clung to me like Velcro. I was the buffer between him and the world he frequently perceived with terror. It was exhausting. Add his little sister to the mix: a fire-cracker ball of defiance. Her mouth wide, fists in her armpits and brow furrowed, her tiny body stoic in a striking figure of intimidation like a frilled neck lizard under attack. My lion-hearted girl felt all the injustices in the world and needed to 'fix' them. Every day was an overwhelming battle. As a single mama, I was working several jobs to keep a roof over our heads. Some days it felt it would be easier to just let the ocean swallow me into the very depths I was working so hard to fight.

> *'Overwhelmed means an extreme level of stress, an emotional and/or cognitive intensity to the point of feeling unable to function.'*
>
> Brene Brown

As an eldest child, I had learned to use perfectionism and mastery of control to manage my own childhood trauma triggers. Embedded in every cell in my body was the idea that I had to 'always get it right' to be worthy of love. It was hard work to always have to be perfect and I often felt alone in my efforts. 'I am not good enough, nor worthy of the effort,' was the broken record playing in my head. I knew that childhood trauma has a way of repeating itself unless we change the way we perceive ourselves. I was desperate to break the cycle, at the very least for my kids' sake. There had to be a better life than this one of fear and trepidation. But still, I did not feel worthy of change.

> **REFLECTION:** Have you ever felt the constant battle to get it right? Have you ever lived in fear that you are never going to be good enough? And what if ... what if there was a better way?

When I look back to my children's younger years, I am acutely aware of the fears that dominated my mindset. Within my mind's eye the shadow of those enormous sharks with rows of white teeth circled below the tiny lifeboat I had created for my children and me. They took so much of my attention and drained my energy out of me. I had no faith in my ability to get us to safety. I felt so much fear rising and falling in my chest like wild surf, that on many days I found it hard to breathe let alone stay above the surface of the frothing water.

Wonder, sandcastles and the power of the pause

When my kids were most rowdy, their emotions too big for their little bodies, I instinctively dropped the chores, gathered them up and added sand and salt water. I came to discover that at the beach, the shackles of my fear were loosened, the kids would play, and I would get a few moments of peace from the loudness of the world. Yet the battle inside my head would rage on. Overthinking, lists, fears, overwhelm.

Then one day, wonder found me.

It started with a small glimpse. I raised my eyes to the sound of my children laughing. I could see my daughter splashing as she scooped the bucket of water, running to her brother and the giant moat around the sandcastle they had built together. I found my breath, and in that moment was aware of something greater than myself: peace. I felt grounded yet *awake* for the first time in years. The noise in my head faded to the distance. It was so powerful, I decided at that very moment to intentionally look for more moments like this.

By its very nature, wonder brings us into the here and now. It is mindful, like a PAUSE button on the universe. A sudden realisation. An unexpected noticing of something so awesome you must take a breath and just take it in. Because here is what I know to be true: our emotions and thoughts are like sharks. When we swim in the ocean, the sharks will be there. When we try to avoid them or fight them off, when we swim away frantically, they will be more likely to chase and attack. But if we notice them, and observe in wonder, most of the time they will pass us by.

So much of our fear (anxiety) and depression is worsened by our steadfastness to our own ideas, ones that prevent us from experiencing the wonders of life. For when you let the fear sit just at arm's length, and put your face under the water, it is peaceful. Gentle bubbles rise from the deep blue, and if you are lucky, the wonder of whale song is heard in the distance.

You can create this pause too, starting with one moment, then training yourself to extend it – so that one day you too can let the fear swim by you, and open yourself up to experience the whale song with wonder and gratitude. This was a lesson I learned with time, repetition, the inspiration of my children, and the support of wondrous women that had walked this path before me. And, if I can do this, then so can you.

> **REFLECTION:** Can you start here, just as I did, and open yourself up to the power of wonder? What are your sandcastle moments, just waiting for you?

Over the years I have discovered that wonder is most easily found in the natural world, and if we can find a moment of quiet (in our minds, as well as our external world), then they start to appear in everyday moments too.

If you want to start, I suggest finding a place in nature and grounding your feet down into the earth or sand. Start with a few deep breaths to quieten your mind, letting the worries of tomorrow and regrets of yesterday pass by like clouds; and then notice the wonder around you – it is truly everywhere: A stormy sky. Waves crashing one after the other. The song of a bird, or two. A rainbow so vivid and broad. Your child's laughter and how they squint their eyes just like you when they smile. The 'purr' of the puppy as he wags his whole body at excitement that we have just come home. A warm, soft morning snuggle with your beautiful kids. The stars sparkling every night. The delicious aroma of freshly brewed coffee. A brilliantly coloured flower on the side of the hiking trail, smiling up at the sun. It's like a space opens in your chest and you feel grounded and inspired all at once. Breathe it in and hold it in your mind's eye.

> To help you create this pause of wonder in under five minutes each day, I have also created a *Grounding in Wonder* meditation just for you.

Seeking and thriving through the salve of wonder

Over the last ten years, I have sought wonder as a salve for both my mental health and my children's. Wonder has allowed me to discover moments of beauty and connection, even in moments of overwhelming fear, when I barely knew if I could survive. It inspired the creation of my internationally recognised programs within *The Wonderful Society*, helping mamas to move out of feeling stuck and frightened, out of their depth in the dark, deep water, and into a supportive community rich with light, love, wonder and wholehearted living.

Since Plato and Aristotle, wonder has been studied as a moment when you cannot fully understand something, and only through exploration can you seek understanding and knowledge. Leading experts in fields of psychology and neuroscience currently agree that these components of observation and openness in wonder provide a means to connection, curiosity and courageous action that are such powerful antidotes to the traumas, fast moving information and overwhelm of emotions in today's world. The sharks are still there, but so too is the whale song.

Wonder brings curiosity, courage and connection that allows you to step into a wholehearted life

Once you start though, be warned the allure of wonder is addictive! And as you welcome it in, the need to fight with the fear, and the feeling of not being worthy, dissipates. Research tells us that emotions that we don't fight with – or avoid – usually pass in 60-90 seconds if we let them be. And wonder was the key for me to be able to drop the fight so the emotions could flow. Wonder took my attention away from the fear, perfectionism and overthinking, bringing me back to the ground and letting me breathe. It allowed me to be present with those I love and start to put together the wonderful, wholehearted life I had always wanted for myself and my kids.

Don't get me wrong, these feelings do continue to rise up, but by staying open to the sense of wonder you can allow the emotions to pass by. You are empowered to focus your energy and attention on what your wholehearted, wonderful life can really be.

> **REFLECTION:** What heavy emotions could you put down if you let more wonder into your world?

I encourage you to invite wonder in. It can be scary at first, but let the wonder carry you, let it create a little space and curiosity, so the feelings flow through you, and though you notice them, they last only for a short while, like the majestic Kalihi swimming past. *'Hello, there you are, Fear.'* [deep breath] *'Can you hear that wondrous whale song? I do hope you have a great day,'* and the emotion has moved by and you can now focus on the melody of whale song.

Wonder, whale song and a wholehearted life

Tuning into a new way of being takes courage. It isn't always easy to hear the calls – and its rhythm changes like the seasons and the ocean. The sharks will still be there, and so too will the whale song. There will be storms and sunny days, and everything in between, all of it with a wonder of its own, if we can just tune in to it.

And my daughter, on that miraculous day, was deeply tuned in. As she climbed out of the water, she was quiet, reverent. Her eyes as big as saucers and her smile seemed to extend into the sparkles of sunshine glinting off the water. She was speechless in her wonder. It took over an hour, a breakfast picnic, and a large coffee before she started talking. There it was: the courageous action inspired by wonder – a future ocean conservationist emerging – born of wonder, and my willingness as her mama to model living a wholehearted, wonderful life, one open to the magic and miracles of wonder.

Chapter Six

From Shadows to Strength

A journey of resilience takes courage, belief, perseverance and connection.

With Cecile Vence: A community leader, Victorian Multicultural Honour Roll inductee (2024), and a highly loved and acclaimed trainer who empowers migrants to develop their communication skills, so they have a voice and find their place in a new country.

'Difficulties in life are intended to make us better, not bitter.'
Dan Reeves

According to the National Archives of Australia, migrants face a range of challenges as they settle into their new lives. These include learning a new language, finding work, a place to live and adjusting to a new culture.

If you are new to Australia, you will probably understand when I say that the journey of transitioning from another country is extremely challenging. My own journey for the betterment of my family has been both daunting and transformative. I never imagined the strength I would need to muster to navigate this huge life change.

My past experiences included an array of struggles that tested my resilience daily. Finding employment was an uphill battle, often filled with rejections and uncertainties despite my qualifications and educational background. In the process, I also embarked on a journey of self-discovery, trying to find my place in a new culture while holding onto my identity. Financial issues were a constant source of stress, as we worked hard to make ends meet in a foreign land.

Amidst these challenges, I also faced domestic issues that added to the emotional and psychological strain. Yet, through every hardship, I discovered an inner strength I never knew I possessed. This strength fueled my determination to overcome obstacles and strive for a better future for my family.

My story is one of resilience, growth, and the unwavering belief that every struggle brings us closer to our true potential. By sharing my journey, I hope to inspire others who may be facing similar challenges and remind them that they are not alone.

My awakening began with a realisation: I am special in my own way.

My parents raised me with love and support, instilling in me the values of respecting the elderly and being genuinely kind to others. My late mum fostered a strong faith within me. Answering back to elders was strictly discouraged. Despite living on an average income, my parents invested in our education by sending me to a prestigious private school known for producing students with strong English communication skills. This was one of my valuable skills which I have carried on throughout my journey.

However, despite a strong foundation and a solid ethos, life was not always easy. When I decided to start my own family and grow personally, the harsh realities of life began to set in. During this time, I struggled with insecurities and a lack of self-confidence, often looking down on myself. The shadows of my past controlled my self-worth. I have experienced verbal abuse, which I never realised was part of domestic issues. I experienced profound feelings of worthlessness, I have been bullied because of my petite physique, my height and being judged by peers I once cared for and supported, lingered in my mind. I felt betrayed and I often found myself in silent reflection, burdened by seemingly insurmountable questions. How did I endure such pain? What inner strength allowed me to rise when everything seemed determined to pull me down? These questions echoed in my mind like persistent whispers, denying me peace.

The past often felt like a prison, confining me in its shadows, a struggle that remained hidden from everyone, including my parents. In our country, family violence is an extremely sensitive topic. Cultural norms and social stigma can perpetuate silence and shame, making it challenging for victims to seek help. Even as I share this now, it is uncomfortable for me, but I believe that part of moving forward is to confront and accept the difficult truths. Because I strongly believe that my past doesn't define me, I am determined to embrace these tough realities and continue my journey towards healing and empowerment.

I knew my story was not yet complete. I continued to breathe, to fight and to embrace the potential for transformation. My strong faith and deep spiritual belief, instilled by my beautiful mother who passed away at the age of 75 in 2023 due to colon cancer, made me aware of a glimmer of hope within me – the hope that someday, I could transform my pain into a source of power.

Your past does not dictate your future

Confronting the past can be intimidating, but it is a crucial step towards creating a brighter future. It starts with acceptance and understanding that it is okay not to be okay. By embracing our flaws and acknowledging past experiences, no matter how bitter, we can find the strength to transform our lives.

Reflecting on my own experiences, I confronted the painful memories I had buried deep inside. The bullying I endured, the hurtful words that cut through me, the judgement from those around me and the feelings of inadequacy were all part of a narrative I had yet to rewrite. These feelings remained bottled up, as I feared that exposing my scars would bring embarrassment to my family. I questioned whether sharing my truth would make me appear weak or unworthy.

I felt the weight of my silence, as I carried these burdens alone. However, a flicker of determination began to emerge. I realised that these feelings were not mine to carry alone. By sharing my story, I hoped to connect with women who felt voiceless, who had endured their own battles in silence.

By speaking out, perhaps I could help lift someone else from their despair?

Cultivating self-belief: The power of positive affirmations

Finding your voice after something like this, is not an overnight journey. For me, it required courage and vulnerability. I began by writing down my thoughts, pouring out the emotions that had long been trapped within me. With every word, I felt a sense of release. I held deeply onto my belief that sharing my experiences would empower others – women who had faced similar challenges, who struggled with self-doubt, and who needed reassurance that they were not alone.

One day, I attended a session on Silva Mind Control and discovered the powerful impact of positive affirmations. *The Silva Mind Control Method, now commonly known as the Silva Method, is a self-help and meditation program developed by José Silva in the 1960s. It aims to enhance an individual's mental abilities through relaxation techniques, development of higher brain functions. The Silva Method includes various techniques to help individuals reprogram their minds for continuous improvement, manage stress, and achieve personal goals. It has been used by millions of people worldwide for personal growth and self-improvement.*

I stood before a mirror and whispered to myself, '*I am enough, I am brave, I am beautiful, and I am a great leader who can lead with love.*' It was a small but significant moment. I knew that if I wanted to inspire others, I first needed to believe in myself. Slowly, I began to embrace my journey and the unique qualities that made me who I am. I sought out communities, both online and offline, where I could connect with others who shared similar experiences. In these spaces, I found a sense of belonging.

Find other beacons of hope

For every issue you are going through, there is someone that has made their way through it, that you can learn from.

In my own quest for empowerment, I was inspired by some remarkable individuals who had faced adversity and emerged triumphant. Alice Pung, whose family fled to Australia, faced challenges as a migrant personally.

Pung is known for her memoirs, novels, essays, and children's books. She is a practicing solicitor, has taught and mentored students both in Australia and internationally. Now a lawyer and a famous writer. Jane Lu, the founder and CEO of Showpo, an online fashion retail company that has grown to generate an approximately $100 million in annual revenue according to my research. Her journey from quitting her corporate job to building a successful business is truly inspiring. In addition to her entrepreneurial success, Jane Lu joined the cast of Shark Tank Australia in 2023 as one of the "sharks," where she invests in and mentors aspiring entrepreneurs. Jane faced several challenges as a migrant in Australia, which she overcame with resilience and determination.

These women showed me that it was possible to rise above one's circumstances. They became beacons of hope, lighting the way for those like me who sought to carve out their paths. Their journeys encouraged me to believe that anything is possible when you put your heart into it. I wanted to be like them, to inspire others and to show that our past does not have to define our future.

Resilience takes courage

On any kind of healing journey, life will test you and it will throw you obstacles designed to give you more courage and more strength.

Arriving in Australia in 2016, the sense of isolation was overwhelming. I felt completely alone in a new land, far from my parents, relatives and friends back in the Philippines. Although my family and children were with me, the weight of my loneliness was compounded by the realisation that my qualifications – a Master's degree in Business Management and a

Bachelor of Science in Psychology – held little value in this place, which I fully understand.

Finding a job felt impossible, especially with a three-year-old daughter to care for and my two sons in high school. I felt a sense of urgency to provide support to my husband who was the breadwinner and who was working so hard to support the family.

Rejection is my biggest fear and each one of these rejections I faced, felt like a reminder of my worthlessness – reinforcing the belief that I was unqualified and unworthy.

Somewhere deep inside however, I knew I was here for more. That I needed to shift my perspective. To make a paradigm shift. To transform my feelings of despair into determination. This is where my strong faith came in, and the mind techniques I learned through the Silva Method again proved handy.

Build your resilience by finding meaning in your life

Despite the anxiety and feelings of worthlessness, I made a conscious decision to focus on finding meaning in my life. I wanted to give back to Australia that had welcomed me and my family. I began volunteering with the Red Cross, bringing my daughter along. This simple act of service became my lifeline. It allowed me to connect with others and cultivated a support network in the community.

Through volunteering, I discovered the transformative power of helping others. I engaged with individuals from diverse backgrounds, sharing stories and building connections. The more I interacted with others, the more I realised that everyone carries their own burdens, their own stories of struggle and triumph. This understanding deepened my empathy and motivated me to continue giving back.

In volunteering, I learned that resilience is often built in community. The stories of those I met inspired me. They had faced their own trials and had emerged stronger. I absorbed their lessons, recognising that adversity can cultivate compassion, strength and understanding. It became clear to me that my struggles could serve a greater purpose if I chose to share them.

Bravely embracing new experiences opens door to different opportunities

I started to view challenges as opportunities for growth. Adopting a growth mindset allowed me to celebrate even the smallest achievements. I set realistic goals for myself, breaking down larger aspirations into manageable steps. Whether it was learning new skills or connecting with others, I focused on progress rather than perfection. *I challenged and competed with myself.*

To navigate my new environment, I committed myself to learning the language and cultural nuances of Australia. Understanding the local jargon and slang was essential for effective communication and I practiced diligently. I attended community events, engaged in conversations and built friendships that enriched my experience.

Acknowledging my journey also meant being open to different opportunities, even if they felt outside my comfort zone. I took on various jobs, each one adding a layer to my resilience. I worked as a kitchen hand, receptionist and occasionally as a cleaner especially when we have staffing shortages, I assisted a good friend in some domestic chores, caring for a child with special needs and eventually in a training role. Each task taught me valuable lessons, whether it was about adaptability, multitasking, teamwork, customer service or time management.

Resilience is often built in community

After a year, my hard work began to pay off. I enrolled in a hospitality course at the Centre for Participation in Horsham, a regional city located in the Wimmera region of western Victoria, which provided me with invaluable skills and knowledge. This opportunity not only allowed me to grow as a person but also opened doors to potential employment, broadening my professional horizons and providing valuable experiences that will benefit my future career.

As I studied, I began to see a clearer path ahead. The experience of learning alongside others who shared similar journeys reinforced my belief that I was not alone. I was hired as a Migrant Liaison Worker, helping others improve their English Language Conversational skills. In this role, I felt a sense of fulfillment and purpose as I supported fellow migrants in their own journeys. I also felt I was back on track, as training has always been my passion.

Through this work, I witnessed the struggles and triumphs of my students. Their stories mirrored my own in many ways. Together, we celebrated each small victory, whether it was mastering a new word or finding a job. In these moments, I realised the importance of community and the strength that comes from sharing experiences.

I continued to spread my wings by volunteering with the Victoria Regional Multicultural Council, serving as a Regional Advisory Council Member and collaborated with the Wimmera Settlement Services. *I have also been very active as a community leader.* Contributing to the betterment of your community can provide a sense of purpose and fulfillment, knowing that you're making a difference.

Resilience and purpose comes from supporting others

If you are feeling lost and worthless, becoming an active participant in your community and supporting others on their journey is a way to feel a part of something and important again.

Over time, my efforts supporting others began to bear fruit. The programs I led were recognised with awards, affirming the positive impact we made together as a community. The support from the organisation and the people around me fueled my passion to continue advocating for migrants and their rights.

Receiving recognition for our work was a turning point for me. It validated my efforts and inspired me to keep pushing forward. I had gone from feeling lost and worthless to becoming an active participant in my community. This transformation was not just about personal growth; it was about giving a voice to those who felt unheard.

In one particularly proud moment, our English Language Conversation program has been highly commended by the Victorian Multicultural Awards for Excellence held at the Government house in 2022 and Micro Business program has been the Finalist of the Victorian Learn Local Pre-Accredited Program Award (For large providers) in 2021 as part of community engagement. It was a testament to the hard work of everyone involved, and I felt an overwhelming sense of gratitude for being part of such a meaningful initiative. This recognition was not just for me but for all the individuals who had come together to support one another.

Empowering others through your story is the way to find fulfillment

As I personally continued to grow, I took on a role as a Mental Health Worker, which provided me with the opportunity to support others in need. Working in this capacity allowed me to expand my skills and further develop my understanding of the challenges faced by migrants and locals alike. I felt empowered to provide essential support to those who were struggling and I dedicated myself to fostering an inclusive environment.

In this role, I encountered individuals grappling with their own anxieties, fears and past traumas. I listened to their stories and offered compassion, drawing from my own experiences to connect with them on a deeper level. I try to become a source of encouragement, reminding them that healing is a journey and that they are not alone in their struggles.

My journey taught me that empowerment is a collective effort. By sharing my story and experiences, I hoped to inspire others to embrace their uniqueness and find their voices. I wanted women, especially those who felt marginalised, to understand that their stories deserve to be told. I assisted a colleague in organising workshops, coffee meetings and support groups, creating safe spaces for dialogue and connection in collaboration with good friends in the community.

A message of hope

To all women who feel unheard or discriminated against: Your journey is important, and your experiences matter. Though it may feel isolating, know that you are not alone. Share your story, embrace your true self, and recognise the strength that resides within you. Your voice has the power to inspire change, to uplift others and to create a sense of belonging.

As I continue on this journey, I remain committed to empowering women and advocating for their rights. Together, we can create a community where everyone feels valued, seen, and heard. The challenges we face may be daunting, but they do not define us. Instead, they shape us into the resilient individuals we are destined to become.

> Always remember that building resilience is essential for everyone, especially if you are a migrant navigating new environments and challenges. Here are some practical tips which I have learned:
>
> **1. Cultivate a Support Network**: Connect with fellow migrants and support groups who can uplift you. Sharing experiences can provide emotional support and valuable resources. Visit local resource centres, neighbourhood houses and libraries to gather more information and for connection.
>
> **2. Embrace a Growth Mindset**: View challenges as opportunities for growth. This mindset helps in adapting to new situations. Change the way you view things. When faced with setbacks, don't give up. Use obstacles as learning experiences. Understand that failure is a part of

the journey toward success.

3. Set Realistic Goals: Break down large goals into manageable steps. Celebrate small wins and achievements to build confidence and motivation. Apply the SMARTER technique. Make your goals specific, measurable, attainable, time based, exciting and rewarding.

4. Learn the Language: Improving language skills can enhance communication and integration. Consider enrolling in language classes to boost your confidence. Additionally, research the local culture and familiarize yourself with local jargons.

5. Stay Connected to Culture: Maintain connections to your cultural roots through community events, food and traditions by attending Cultural Diversity programs. This can provide comfort and a sense of belonging. Connect with the ones whom you trust.

6. Practice Self-Care: Prioritise physical and mental well-being through regular exercise, healthy eating and mindfulness activities. Taking care of oneself enhances resilience. Explore different activities you enjoy, like sports, arts, music, or dancing.

7. Be Open to New Experiences: Step out of our comfort zone and challenge yourself. Be open to upskilling, willing to undergo a career transition and ready to apply your transferable skills. This openness can lead to new friendships and opportunities for personal and professional growth.

8. Seek Professional Help When Needed: If feeling overwhelmed, reach out to counselors or mental health professionals. This kind of support can provide coping strategies and guidance. Never be afraid to ask for help and support.

9. Educate Yourself: Learn about your rights and available resources in your new country. Being informed, empowers you to navigate systems more effectively. The library became my closest companion when I was new to Australia. Be open to learning, research and ask questions.

10. Practice Patience and Perseverance: Recognise that adapting to a new environment takes time. Be patient and kind to yourself. Stay committed to *your goals, even when faced with setbacks.* This is where positive self talk comes in.

11. Develop Problem-Solving Skills: Approach challenges with a solution-oriented mindset. Break down problems into smaller parts and brainstorm possible solutions. Develop a creative mindset and solicit feedback from peers. *When overwhelmed, reach out and ask for help.*

12. Follow my signature 5 Cs for Building Resilience as a migrant: Please follow the QR code to my website where you find more info about my 5 Cs for Building Resilience as a migrant: Communicate, cultivate a positive mindset, contribute, collaborate and commit.

Embrace your shadows to find your strength and power

Reflecting on my journey, I realise that I have come full circle. From a place of pain and isolation to one of empowerment and connection, I have discovered the beauty of resilience. I have learned to embrace my past while also recognising that it does not dictate my future. I have found strength in vulnerability, courage in sharing my truth and purpose in supporting others.

As I move forward, I carry with me the lessons learned, the friendships forged and the hope that resides in each of us. I have learned to choose my battles. I am committed to making a difference, not just for myself but for all those who share this beautiful, complex journey of life.

In sharing my story, I open the door for others to do the same. Together, we can create a world where every voice is valued, every story is honoured and every person has the opportunity to thrive. Remember, you can be who you want to be, as long as you believe in yourself. Now, I am ready to face the future, knowing that I am special in my own way and that my journey is just beginning.

Acknowledgements

A huge thank you to Adie McDermott for inviting me to be part of the 'Lead with Love' book. This opportunity has truly broadened my horizons and allowed me to embrace and accept myself in ways I never imagined. The training, along with the genuine connection she has shown, has helped me immensely. Adie's vision and support have inspired me deeply and I'm grateful to have been part of this journey. Thank you for believing in me and for creating a space where we can all lead with love. Forever grateful.

I would also like to extend my heartfelt gratitude to my late mother who has been my rock, my ever-supportive dad, my siblings, my lovely children, my spouse, my trusted relatives and family friends back home in the Philippines, in Australia and other parts of the world, my mentors, employers and of course to my fellow migrants. A special thanks to the Centre for Participation, Wimmera Settlement Services and Victorian Multicultural Commission – Regional Advisory Council, for granting me the privilege and wonderful opportunity to continue my advocacy in leading and supporting migrants.

References

- National Archives of Australia, Migrant stories https://www.naa.gov.au/search?search_api_fulltext=about+migrants

- The Silva Mind Control Method https://silvamethod.com/the-silva-mind-control-method

- Go For It - The Incredible story of Jane Lu https://medium.com/women-of-inspiration/go-for-it-the-incredible-story-of-showpo-ceo-jane-lu-afdee02af8a1

- The Goodreads choice awards Final Round https://www.goodreads.com/book/show/1182481.Unpolished_Gem

- https://www.alicepung.net/books/

Chapter Seven

Wild Seasons: Cycling through change

Nurture personal transformations, create inner resilience and hope with the rhythms of nature as your guide.

> With author, homeopath and functional medicine practitioner, bridging the paradigm gap between energy medicine, lifestyle and nutrition science – Nicole Cullinan.

Do you still believe in magic? Remember when you were a child and you believed that fairies, monsters and Father Christmas existed? Maybe you had an imaginary friend or like me put your cat in doll's clothes for a tea party and invited a queen? I used to love picking flowers, playing dress up and making tasty treats for such tea parties. I still adore the illustrated flower fairy books by Cicely Mary Barker. Childhood was a sacred time when wild imaginations are encouraged, and messy creative play is entertained. Living in the moment was easy!

So, what happened to all that uninhibited, wild spirit and magical thinking?

Naturally we grow up. The process of 'unbelieving' is sadly often an unavoidable one. Life happens ... social conditioning, disappointments, change, trauma, illness, loss ... plus the reality of living in a concrete jungle with digital workspaces and eating mainly processed foods inform our evolution. Or triggered by a dramatic life change, we might suddenly find ourselves disconnected from the natural world outside of us and separated from our true nature and adventurous spirits.

My darkest days came after we immigrated and I was grieving the loss of my old life. Getting back into bed after dropping the kids at school. Avoiding going to the shops or anywhere where I would encounter people. I was a stranger in a strange land, rudderless, drifting and bewildered. Not being able to communicate effectively because of a language barrier. Hypersensitive to that look of confusion on their faces when I opened my mouth to speak. Being treated like I was stupid because my command of the language was clumsy. Unemployed and not able to work in my profession. It was easier to stay in bed.

I cycled through isolation, a hopeless, dark depression and feelings of disconnection by finding wisdom and a healing balm in the changing seasons, nature, plants and of all things ... *weeds!*

If you are sick, stuck or life throws you an unexpected curveball and you are forced to change, adapt and grow in a harsh and unfamiliar environment without obvious support, or the necessary skills to survive and thrive again, don't give up hope.

Lyanda Lynn Haupt, in her book Rooted says, '*Cutting-edge science supports a truth that poets, artists, mystics, and earth-based cultures across the world have proclaimed over millennia: life on this planet is radically inter-*

connected.' She also says, *'At the crossroads of science, nature, and spirit we find true hope.'*

WE ARE NATURE for all our sophistication, and we are still wild. I know for sure from my own experience, that recovering our wild nature is a vitality that can restore our resilience and a sense of belonging in the world.

Have you ever looked back on your life's events and seen with the clarity of hindsight how it was all connected? Synchronicity, resonance and intuition are the magic of adulthood. This story is how a regular, mindful connection with nature, the power of a human and animal bond, together with the wisdom and ingenuity in plants started a healing journey, discovering self-acceptance and unearthing my creativity in the process. This in turn gave me the strength to rebirth my career, create an online health platform, Wellness Place International and write a book series called Wild Seasons. In essence, *to do what I love* – to continue to educate health seekers by bridging the gap between age-old healing wisdom and conventional medical approaches.

Read on and follow my suggestions if you want to heal by cultivating a new relationship with nature around you and transform your diet and lifestyle by rewilding what you eat and the medicine you use. Your physical and mental health will improve and so will your life. I know this for a fact because it happened to me ... *and it feels like magic!*

Cycling through fear and trauma

We can develop disease, chronic emotional and physical health problems when for whatever reason, we deny who we are and our reliance on plants and animals in our ecosystem. In my practice and personal life, I have frequently seen how it can take a chronic illness or health crisis to make changes and reconnect with your true self and feel rooted and secure again. But to experience a healing transformation, first you need to take stock of how you got to this place in your life. Here is my process …

I was born and bred in South Africa. In 2016 we, my husband, our two (then) children and I immigrated to The Netherlands. It was a gut wrenching decision which we made with our heads and not our hearts because we feared for our lives and children's future. Superficially we had an idyllic life, but in reality, it felt like being in an abusive relationship and very difficult to leave. We did leave after wrestling with the decision for many years, but to my bewilderment, fear followed me.

It wasn't until about two years after we immigrated that I realised this. It became poignantly clear one night while cycling home alone in the dark, returning from a late networking event in the city centre. Riding bicycles almost everywhere and in all weather is very Dutch and so different from South Africa, where I was even driving 400m to take the kids to school as it was the norm and necessity to drive absolutely everywhere. But not at night and definitely not alone at night. So, to tell the truth, I was very unaccustomed to being out on my own at night.

It was close to midnight, and the streets were dark, but well lit. It was quiet and all calm, with only the occasional cyclist or dog walker about. I felt coolness on my cheeks, ears and fingers and there was a wet scent of the early dew in the air. But my heart was pounding in my chest and I was breathing hard because I was pushing myself and cycling fast as if being chased by an invisible attacker. I guess everyone is running from something – their shadow, their past, the fear of dying or losing the ones we love?

Or was it the exhilaration one feels at doing something thrilling and risky – *'Am I actually doing this? Alone? At night? And on a bike?'* My fear response was instinctive and a default set point to which my physiology had habituated. I had to remind myself... *'It's ok, I live in the so-called first world now'*. The realisation hit me, that I had been looking over my shoulder and on high alert my whole life.

This feeling of not having to fear for my safety or life was my first experience of true personal freedom. I could take in this wonderful 'normal' scene and breathe and just be.

Resilience as practice and process

I was physically safe but still not at home in my own skin. We were still profoundly homesick and feeling uprooted as a family. This was a period of painful awakening to the losses and gains of our move.

Around the same time, I got a dog and started walking her in the forest every day. I was captivated by the changing natural environment and how the seasons were like distinct artistic entities with their own palette of colours. I walked the same route twice daily which felt like a walking meditation. I noticed the plants and started to recognise many of them as medicinal and edible wild plants from my studies and clinical practice. The first being stinging nettle, then its antidote dock, elderflowers, fields of wildflowers like poppies, chamomile, cornflowers and St John's wort. It felt like a revelation and I began to crave the calm I felt when out walking and plant watching!

This is the power of the '*Phytoneuroendocrine system,*' a newly coined term by Dr Deanna Minich. It is '*... the complex network of interactions* *between phytochemicals found in plants and the human neuroendocrine system, influencing neurotransmitter production, hormone regulation, and overall neuroendocrine function. It embodies the bidirectional communication pathways between plants and humans, highlighting the therapeutic potential of plant-based interventions in modulating human health and well-being[1].'*

As well as being a vital source of food, plants were our first medicines, and they have been part of the human story by connecting humans and their environment since the beginning of time. The plants became like a new community which provided much needed physiological support to my shattered nervous system. I discovered that resilience building is a practice and process in which plants and even weeds can play a pivotal role.

Cycling through the seasons

In forests I feel the magic of this interconnection especially strongly. Imagine if doctors prescribed 'nature time' instead of, or together with pharmaceutical drugs. To support that idea, a UK Study in 2019[2] revealed that people who spend at least 2 hours per week in nature report significantly better health and wellbeing. There is furthermore a growing body of evidence supporting forest therapy as effective in improving hypertension, stress, and mental-health disorders, such as depression and anxiety[3] and even immune function[4]. I say just walk in the forest, don't wait for that prescription.

By spending time in green and blue natural spaces and eating a diverse seasonal plant-based diet containing edible wild plants[5] you can experience the seasons as a metaphor for the cycle of creation and destruction that is healthy living, one that honours nature's intelligence. Winter is like death, but it is also like a womb. If you withdraw and hibernate for the cold dark months, you can harness energy for the next phase. Spring is like a rebirth, a new beginning and chance for exponential growth. Summer is abundance, flowers, and fruit. Autumn is about maturation, ageing and letting go. When you embrace this cycle and philosophy, you find more authenticity, inner peace and self-acceptance. You also realise that there is a time for everything and discomfort is fleeting and will not last forever. When growing pains persist, it is often because one is resisting natural processes and the greater circular economy.

Like a butterfly's metamorphosis, change and personal transformation can be excruciating and involve loss and really test your ability to adapt and level of resilience. I think the words of Pablo Picasso capture this process well: *'Every act of creation is first an act of destruction'*.

Moving through the cycles of distinct seasons by walking the well-worn forest paths and including in my diet the edible and medicinal plants I encountered, helped me to adapt and make sense of our life's events. I still to this day find it difficult to explain the kinship I feel with the natural world, and especially the native plants of my new home. Except that the familiarity is in my DNA, my ancestral heritage and that my migration back to the birthplace of my ancestors was no coincidence.

Plantfulness is a lifestyle choice

Artist and writer Julia Rose Bower says, *'Plantfulness is a way of living alongside plants intentionally, mindfully and fully appreciative of the ways in which they enrich our lives'*.

I say when life gives you weeds, it's a sign to go for a walk, hug a tree, pick some wildflowers, make something beautiful, edible, medicinal, and wholesome like tea, wild pesto and a creative mezze platter of interesting ingredients and throw in some edible flower petals! Go on, go wild ... *follow the seasons and the magic!*

Here's how to create your own Plantfulness lifestyle

1. **Intention**: Make a conscientious intention to have a daily healing ritual involving plants, nature or any natural elements for the purpose of bolstering your resilience.

2. **Journal:** Journaling your process and having a regular practice of putting your thoughts on paper can be cathartic and give clarity.

3. **Immersion**: Immerse yourself in nature every day and surround yourself with plants. For example, walk in a forest, swim in the sea, work in the garden, have indoor plants and cut flowers in your home, eat your fruit and veggies.

4. **Ritualise**: Create daily rituals for yourself ...
   – Try a walking meditation just looking at plants. Follow the same path every day and notice the plants, name them if you can and watch how the landscape changes over time.
   – Anchor and ground yourself by regularly walking barefoot on as many natural surfaces as you can find.
   – Drink herbal teas made from ethically foraged or seasonal ingredients from your own garden.

5. **Plant foods are like medicine:** Follow a plant-based diet based

on the traditional Mediterranean[6] or Planeterranean[7] diet but using local produce and edible wild plant foods that are in season and indigenous to your area.

6. **Respect nature**: Grow your own kitchen garden or veggie patch and plant the edible wild plants and wildflowers that you love. Look after your environment. The remedies for our illnesses and maladies often lie around us as the plants in our immediate environment.

7. **Personalise your diet and lifestyle and ask for professional help:** Please note that the information in this chapter is not intended to diagnose illnesses or replace the advice of a qualified health professional. I can in no way be held responsible for any adverse effects and negative consequences that arise from ingesting wild plants or using medicinal products made from them, or for errors in plant identification and self-diagnosis. Please seek help if you are concerned about your health and for accurate plant identification.

If you are ready to rediscover plant magic in your life and heal, follow the QR code, to find my Plantfulness Lifestyle Guide, a bunch of other free resources and get access to my community and services.

References

1. The Phytoneuroendocrine System: Connecting Plants to Human Systems Biology - PMC

2. Spending at least 120 minutes a week in nature is associated with good health and wellbeing | Scientific Reports

3. The Psychological and Physical Effects of Forests on Human Health: A Systematic Review of Systematic Reviews and Meta-Analyses - PubMed

4. The Effects of Forest Therapy on Immune Function - PMC

5. Wild Edible Plants: A Challenge for Future Diet and Health - PMC

6. Mediterranean Wild Edible Plants: Weeds or "New Functional Crops"? - PMC

7. Towards a 'Planeterranean' Diet

Chapter Eight

Who Says I Can't Draw?

Examining and challenging fear and the beliefs we tell ourselves.

> With experiential artist and all-round wise woman Mara Chambers.

For 64 years, I held onto the belief that I couldn't draw. This belief wasn't just a passing thought; it was a deeply entrenched story that stayed with me for multiple decades. *'You can't draw'* echoed in my head every time I put pen to paper, even though it was something I had always secretly longed to master. I marvelled at beautiful paintings in galleries, and I envied my friends who called themselves artists – but every time I tried to draw all I could see were childish scratches grazing the page. I started avoiding all scenarios that involved making art, for fear of embarrassment. No Pinot and Picasso classes for me!

But where did this belief come from? Was it based on any real evidence, or was it an assumption I had made about myself without ever really questioning it?

As it turns out, it was the latter.

The silent saboteur

Fear is the opposite of love! Fear is the voice in our heads that says, *'You can't do this,'* or *'This is too dangerous,'* even when the actual threat is minimal or non-existent.

According to *The Handbook of Social Psychology*: *'Fear is an emotional response to perceived threats that triggers a range of psychological changes, including heightened alertness, increased heart rate, and release of stress hormones. These changes prepare the individual for behavioural responses such as fight-or-flight, which involve either confronting the threat or evading it.'*

For many of us, the silent saboteur called *fear* has become second nature. Whether it's avoiding public speaking, steering clear of deep water, or shying away from new experiences, our fears can prevent us from pushing ourselves into enriching experiences that life has to offer. We say, *'I can't do that!'* without ever really trying. We might think this habit is keeping us *safe*, but it sadly *holds us back* from learning new things and living a full and vibrant life.

Questioning assumptions about ourselves

For me, it's not just about my fear of art. Over the years, I've accumulated an embarrassingly long list of things I'm afraid of. These range from the everyday, like dogs or fast cars, to bigger fears like public speaking or trying new things. I had always told myself, *'I can't swim in deep water; I'll drown!'* or *'I don't like heights, but I'm not sure why.'* These were stories I had accepted as true without ever really looking deeply at them.

What do you believe that you can't do – and how true is this limiting belief?

An assumption is an unexamined belief – something we think is true without even *realising* we're thinking it. Our conclusions on everything are based on our assumptions, and if we don't take the time to examine them, we can end up basing our lives on ideas that are totally misguided. Dr. Richard Paul, a leading scholar on critical thinking in the U.S., said that *'critical thinking is thinking about your thinking while you're thinking in order to make your thinking better.'* To truly understand ourselves and the world around us, we must be willing to question the assumptions that underpin our thoughts and actions.

Examine your beliefs, and be the change

This idea became crystal clear to me during an experiential symposium hosted by *Be the Change* in 2006. It was a day that started like any other but ended up changing my life. By lunchtime, I was overwhelmed with emotion, grappling with the environmental impact humans were having on the world. Just listening to Annie Leonard, author of *The Story of Stuff*, say on a huge screen, *'There is no such thing as 'away'. When we throw anything away, it must go somewhere,'* made me realise the depth of my unexamined assumptions about consumption and waste.

By 4pm, I resurfaced with a powerful realisation: I could make a change in this world. But to do so, I had to start by examining the assumptions that had been guiding my actions – both the big ones, like my environmental impact, and the small ones, like my belief that I couldn't draw.

Challenging yourself to try something new

Once I recognised that my life was being governed by unexamined assumptions, I knew I had to start challenging them. I began by focusing on my belief that I couldn't draw. I decided to stretch myself just a little and see what would happen if I pushed against this assumption.

This process wasn't easy. My mind was full of stories about what I could and couldn't do, and these stories were deeply entrenched. But I realised that many of these stories were based on assumptions that I had never questioned.

I started with simple exercises that challenged me to be OK with imperfection on the page – because the point was this: I shouldn't have to be perfect! I would hold a piece of paper and draw for three minutes without looking at the paper on my lap. After three minutes I would peer down at my page and see something that actually looked pretty fascinating – albeit wonky and wobbly, but there was always something I liked!

You might like to write down one fear or limiting belief you have. Ask yourself: Is this belief based on a real experience or an unexamined assumption? Challenge this belief by taking a small step towards confronting it. As you begin to immerse in the activity, you might find that your self-judgements were based on nothing more than fear: fear of failure, fear of the unknown, fear of being judged. But as you push against these fears, you'll begin to see them for what they really are: barriers you have built in your own mind, just as I had.

We often inherit societal expectations or internalise others' judgements, leading to self-doubt. But by questioning these assumptions, you can learn – and lead others – with authenticity.

1. **Identify Assumptions:** Write down the assumptions you've made about your abilities. Are they based on past experiences or societal expectations?

2. **Challenge Them:** For each assumption, ask yourself, 'Is this really true?' Consider how you might challenge these beliefs by stepping into situations that make you uncomfortable.

Becoming a lifelong student of art (or anything)

As I began to challenge my fears, I discovered that learning is wonderful, and life is about experiences! I first began art classes in 2022 and now consider myself both an artist *and a student of art*, embracing every new lesson with enthusiasm and curiosity.

At the same time I started art classes, someone said a passing statement to me about art that gave me mental confidence in this area for the first time in my life: *art is all about maths.* Whether this statement is right or wrong isn't important. What's important is that I made a powerful realisation: *'I like maths. I'm good at maths. Maybe I could merge art with maths? Angles, shapes ... drawing can't be that hard after all!'*

Embracing the role of a lifelong student is key to continuous growth. It's not about having all the answers, but about being open to learning, adapting, and evolving. Maybe you'd like to start experimenting with art – or environmental work – or working with animals! Whatever it is, remember, you can only try, and you can only get better with practice.

I encourage you to seek mentorship, like I did, by finding teachers who can guide you and share their experiences. Always stay curious: never stop asking questions and seeking new perspectives. This keeps your courage and knowledge fresh, and your leadership strong.

From limitation to celebration

Why not reframe your fears – from limitation to celebration? As the philosopher and psychologist William James said, *'The greatest discovery of my generation is that a human being can alter his life by altering his attitudes.'* By changing the way we think about our fears, we can begin to see them not as insurmountable obstacles, but as challenges to be met and overcome. For me, this meant taking a different approach to drawing. Instead of always telling myself, *'I can't draw,'* I began to see drawing as a skill I could develop. I started with small, manageable exercises that allowed me to build confidence and gradually push against the limits I had set for myself.

Nowadays, I call myself an experiential artist with an extra special interest in saving the environment – all due to those words of Annie Leonard. I reuse canvases that have been abandoned or discarded – those meant for hard rubbish, and I have explored how I can re-use these and create an image that gives the canvas a new life. I also use items from packaging to re-use as collage for future projects. *Reduce, re-use, recycle, repair* is my motto!

I also use things like spare bike parts to create 3D art pieces. I used a set of circular gears to represent the sun. In another landscape I used a CD to represent the moon. Being experiential, half the fun is exploring. I couldn't imagine my life now without art in it – it's just so much fun!

Today I am so passionate and supportive of artists new to this field of environmental creativity. I am encouraging and willing to listen to how they feel about their art process. We are all constantly stretching and moulding ourselves while learning new skills.

So, what are you ready to achieve in life? What burning dream do you hold inside? Don't forget to view mistakes as learning opportunities, because, as I discovered, each mistake is a chance to learn and become better. More importantly, celebrate small wins! Acknowledge and celebrate every step you take toward overcoming your fears.

Exercises to kickstart your art

Now that you understand how I began to examine and question fear and step into life as an artist, here are some exercises that helped me live more in love than fear, and of course also to learn to draw. I hope they'll help you too:

EXERCISE 1: Blind Contour Drawing

1. Grab a pencil and a piece of paper.

2. Sit comfortably and choose an object to focus on.

3. Without looking at your paper, draw the object for three minutes.

4. Don't worry about perfection; just let your hand move freely.

5. When you're done, look at your drawing. Find something you like about it – maybe the loose lines or the authentic details. This exercise helps challenge the perfectionist within and encourages playful exploration with creation!

6. Start again with a new subject. Why not try drawing the dog as he

sleeps in front of the fire? Stretch yourself and make it fun at the same time.

EXERCISE 2: Mindful Meditation with Art

1. Find a quiet place to sit comfortably. Have a pen and paper on hand.

2. Close your eyes and focus on these four words: Love, Gratitude, Connection, Self-Love.

3. For each word, spend a few minutes feeling its presence in your heart and then extend that feeling outward to others.

4. Draw on paper the images that came to mind – colours, symbols, faces etc.

5. This meditation can help you question and transform the limiting mind chatter that holds you back.

Embrace the artful imperfections of life

Remember, overcoming fear isn't about being perfect – it's about giving things a go, trying something new, and forming your own opinions based on experience. Don't let unexamined assumptions limit your potential! Embrace courage and continue learning something new every day. By leading with love and examining your old beliefs, you'll not only transform your own life but also inspire and uplift those around you – after all, the world needs all our unique gifts!

Chapter Nine

Just for Today

Gently creating change in your life, one day at a time.

> With creator of *Lead with Love* Adie McDermott.

If you would like to transform or create change in your life, changing something 'forever' may at first seem too huge, especially as we now know through scientific studies that our nervous systems and minds do not like change, even if it is for the good. In fact they both prefer to live with 'familiar' chaos, unhappiness or hell than move to an 'unfamiliar' place of peace, happiness, fulfilment or love, and they throw up so many roadblocks to change. That is exactly why, inspired by the 5 principles of Reiki, I developed this *Just For Today* process. A process of change that feels achievable, and allowable one day at a time.

It is widely said (and I totally believe) that if you want to change the world, you need to change yourself first. In-turn, I believe that to create the most beautiful, joyful, authentic and full of love type life, you need to be comfortable to totally be and express yourself. This takes self-acceptance and self-compassion. A major shift in how you think about yourself and your life.

We don't do many things in life without thinking and yet thinking has a habit of holding us back. You don't feel good enough because you think you are not, you worry or feel anxious because you think you do, you feel pain or fear because you think you do and if your life sucks it is most probably because you think it does. The good news is thinking can be controlled and that you can change how you think and what you focus on.

Two people that come to mind to illustrate the enormous power of our minds to survive great suffering and trauma are Viktor Frankl and Edith Eger, both survivors of Nazi prison camps during one the most evil times in the world has ever known, The Holocaust. If you like you can read more about how Edith found meaning in suffering and now teaches others freedom from their thoughts, in her books the Choice and Gift, or start by watching her YouTube interview with Oprah Winfrey. (You will find the link in the story resources).

There are so many ways we can change our thinking and we work through my favourites in all my self-expression programs, creative wellness courses and honestly, even my art classes.

Today I would like to talk about the 5 Reiki principles/ideals and how they can help transform your whole life (and your art too if you like) one day at a time. I will also introduce you to a meditation you can do that uses these principles or ideas as mantras.

There is nothing not to love about the Reiki principles. What I truly love about them however is they are so simple and so beautiful and if everyone practiced them daily, the world would truly be a better place. Secondly, they teach us also to live in the day, to be more in the present. And lastly but not least I LOOOVE the fact that you only have to commit to them for one day at a time. After all, committing to something for a lifetime is something our mind resists, while committing to one day at a time however is easy.

Let's face it, changing your life, how you feel about yourself and releasing and changing beliefs you have carried around about yourself all your life is not an easy task. It takes years to do. Healing is like an onion. There are so many layers to it. You take off one layer and there is another underneath.

It doesn't help either that our minds actually don't like change. They don't like change or to be out of control and feel safer remaining the way that they are, even if that is unhealthy and debilitating. You may have found through healing work you do that your mind puts up roadblocks to feeling good about yourself. Your mind and your negative thoughts become stronger before they get better. It may try to tell you (even louder than normal) that what you are doing is not right and that you could never be how you are saying you want to be. I have found this many times and have sometimes found it really frightening, but I have learnt that if you hold onto the fact that *'your thoughts are not the truth'* no matter what they are saying about you and keep going through this, you do get to the other side.

Although it is widely talked about, Tara Brach and Ekhart Tolle are two modern proponents of the theory that our thoughts are not the truth and don't make us who we are. And how being in the moment, the NOW not the past or the future is the way to freedom from our minds. Yes you heard that right ... *FREEDOM FROM OUR MINDS!*

They also talk a lot about how watching your thoughts instead of paying attention to them is the way to free yourself. I love the theory that thoughts are like clouds. They come and go in our minds and we do not need to pay attention to them all, in fact we have so many (up to 60,000 per day) that we can't and so we have a choice which ones we listen to and give power to.

I have spent many years healing from intrusive thoughts, self-loathing, negativity and limited beliefs. I have learnt a lot along the way from healers around the world. I have also tried out many things. Energy healing is something that I totally recommend, things like yoga, breathwork, acupuncture, cranial osteopathy or Reiki. I have found Reiki, Yin Yoga and Breathwork to be so powerful in helping me to shift old beliefs, stuckness and emotions, feel good about myself, less reactive to things around me, and less concerned with what others think of me that I have studied them all so I can use them to support others to gently heal what is standing in the way of a joyful life and their greatest self-expression.

For today however, I would like to introduce you to the 5 Reiki principles or Ideals and share with you a meditation you can do that uses these principles or ideas as mantras in a meditative state. What I love about doing them in a meditative state is that this is the most absorbable, mind-altering state to be in and you will start to implement the things you are saying very quickly.

The original principles written by Mikoa Usui have been adapted in a few different ways but basically go like this:

Just for today I will not anger

Just for today I will not worry

Just for today I will be grateful for all that I have

Just for today I will do honest work

Just for today I will be kind to all living creatures.

It sometimes does not come naturally to live without anger, worry, live with gratitude, to do your best work and be kind to every living creature. As I mentioned earlier, your mind and nervous system may not even like the idea of it. If you say the mantra to yourself every morning or every evening it does however start to train you in a gentle way to catch yourself not doing these things and stop them. In the past worry has been a big one for me, and so if I feel myself worrying I can simply say, '*Just for today I will not worry*' and the anxiety and worry lifts and I automatically feel calm in my body. This also helps in the middle of the night, when thinking and worrying about something that hasn't even happened yet is keeping you from sleeping.

The best past is ANYTHING else you want to change in your life or give up, can be added to this list:

Just for today I will to be kind to myself

Just for today I will allow myself to be imperfect

Just for today I will allow myself to dream big

Just for today I will love myself like I am the most precious and valuable being on this earth

Just for today I will live as if there is no tomorrow

Just for today I allow myself to receive

Just for today I allow myself to be heard, valued and loved

Just for today ... insert what you want or need here.

A link to a 5 Reiki principles mediation by Tiara Wiggins and 4 Wise Monkeys can be found in the story resources. If you want to use your own, you will get the quickest results by reciting them in a very relaxed brain state, when you first wake up in the morning, right before you go to sleep and of course during meditation.

Resources

- Edith Eger interview
  https://www.oprah.com/own-super-soul-sunday/dr-edith-eva-eger-the-choice

- 5 Reiki principles meditation
  https://www.youtube.com/watch?v=p_gIaVvOKi0

- More about the 5 reiki principles
  https://www.souladvisor.com/your-sanctuary/article/what-are-the-5-principle-of-reiki-that-promote-wellness

TUNING INTO YOUR HEART AND SOUL

Spiritual development stories and
processes that connect you
back to your heart and
your soul so you rediscover
who you truly and innately are.

Chapter Ten

HeartWriting: Your heart always holds the answers

Find your authentic creative voice, express yourself fearlessly and start living your wildest dreams.

> With best-selling author and magazine editor, healer and creator of the world recognised HeartWriting method, Rose Mascaro.

Do you remember what it was like to be a child, whipping up magic potions in your backyard, painting whacky masterpieces, and orchestrating wild musicals? What a time to be alive – those years of unbridled creativity! For me, my childhood was spent under the jacaranda tree creating all kinds of weird and marvellous things. I wrote a series of books, and after charging my family 20 cents a pop, I knew *I was a real author.*

So what happened to all that creative childhood promise? Maybe you also dreamt of being an artist, a dancer, a singer, a story writer, a musician – and perhaps, like me, you ditched your dreams after being told that 'artists don't make money, sweetheart.' Maybe as a teen you succumbed to the pressure of societal success – exams, jobs, responsibilities. The truth is, once our brains speed up with the stresses of life, it's so much harder to enter those soft and spacious creative worlds like we used to.

Many years into an unfulfilling, uncreative career, I stumbled into a yoga class with a sore neck and a sorry list of woes. In savasana meditation, something cracked open inside me and *I remembered my childhood dreams.* With the scent of incense and the soft hum of Indian instruments, my heart spoke – and for the first time as an adult, I could see the truth of my life. *You are going to be a writer, and you're going to work with other writers, and you are going to travel the world with your words.* Ever since, I've never looked back – and my life has erupted into a blaze of creative magic.

Let me tell you today – do *not* give up on your dreams. Just as Liz Gilbert, author of *Big Magic* tells us, you *can* and *should* live a life of fearless creativity: 'I'm talking about living a life that is driven more strongly by curiosity than by fear.' You *can* succeed at your craft, you *can* change people's lives in creative ways; you *can* live outside of a 9-5 job; and you *can* travel the whole world doing it. I know this, because I now do! But back on that fateful day in yoga class, I was a writer *who wasn't writing*. I had buried myself deep into my work and I'd completely forgotten my dreams that had sung their truth to me when I was a little girl – until this glorious moment when I awakened.

The voice that spoke to me so loudly during that class? It was my heart, unlocked by deep meditation. I listened to its message and clutched the pages of its promises to my chest – and two years later I was officially a paid writer and magazine editor. Two years after that, I launched my dream writing workshops for adult writers *with heart,* and so it's no wonder I named my business *HeartWriting.*

Unpacking the boxes that block your heart

To hear the voice of my heart, first I needed to unpack the boxes of baggage that had been weighing me down for so long. Maybe you also have a dream to live more authentically and creatively from the heart – and maybe you don't know where to start. Listening to the spiritual powerhouse inside you isn't easy when there are boxes of heavy baggage stacked high around your heart.

Think of it like this: Inside us is a beautiful golden passage that leads to the truth in your heart. When we travel through this passage without fear, we can achieve anything, because we are guided by love – and love makes anything possible. But when we accumulate old hurts, we store them secretly, and here's where it gets tricky – we can't see through the passage anymore. We can't venture through to the heart; there are too many boxes. Hell, we don't even know what this passage *represents* anymore. We are blocked from self-love. And when we don't believe in ourselves, we can't make our dreams materialise.

Sifting through the boxes of pain

I became a writer only after clearing out those painful old boxes and making radical space in my heart. It meant confronting and feeling the pain of my past that was blocking me from my dreams. In her book *Radical Acceptance,* Tara Brach says, 'When we stop fighting against the pain, we can begin to open ourselves to the freedom that lies beyond it.'

So, I began the process of sifting through the pain. I revisited the limiting beliefs that had haunted me since childhood – careless comments like, 'You can only make it as an artist if you're extremely talented or lucky.' What I discovered was that it didn't feel safe to be a writer, because I had to be the best – *or else*. I also discovered that my parents had big dreams that hadn't been realised. Both had subconsciously passed on their feelings of fear, failure and 'it's just not possible' on to me.

According to Dr. Claire Weekes in *Self-Help for Your Nerves*, it's helpful to face your fears using these simple steps:

1. Face (don't run away)

2. Accept (don't fight against)

3. Float (don't freeze)

4. Let time pass (let go of impatience)

By facing and accepting my old hurts and generational fears, I could finally let them go and move forward towards my dreams of being a writer. My therapist showed me that the answers were within me, but it takes courage to turn on the light, face the pain, and create lasting change. Therapy helped me rewire unconscious beliefs and confront childhood traumas, clearing the path for my creative spirit to shine.

Make space (using the theta brainwave)

Facing fears is one thing, but creating space for success is another. Scientific studies show that regular meditation promotes creativity-enhancing heart coherence, cognitive flexibility and innovative thinking. Another fascinating discovery about meditation is that it increases alpha and theta brainwave activity, both linked to creativity and artistic flow. But slowing down and creating *space* is the key.

The theta brainwave is specifically associated with subconscious access and deep artistic insight, but we can only access this state on the cusp of sleep. Thomas Edison, the great inventor of the lightbulb, knew this theory well, and he *made space* to access the theta state (and his best new ideas) simply by resting in an armchair. Imagine if you could harness your brain's creative potential while drifting off to sleep, waking up with your next great idea just waiting for you. Sounds like magic, right? Well, that's exactly what Edison did – and you can too, with a little twist of your own.

Thomas Edison would settle into a chair, holding a ball in his hand. As he began to nod off, the ball would eventually slip from his grasp and clatter to the floor, waking him up. Right at that moment, he was often struck by flashes of insight – those 'aha!' moments we all crave as creatives. It turns out Edison was tapping into the theta brainwave state, that dreamy, in-between phase where the mind drifts freely, unbound by the rigid rules of conscious thought. In this state, creativity flows like a river, washing away the debris of doubt and overthinking, leaving behind pure, unfiltered thought and imagination.

What if you could use this technique to boost your own creativity? Maybe you don't have to hold a ball – what if you tried meditating instead, slipping into that same relaxed, theta-rich state? Could you tap into that deep well of inspiration to find the perfect words or ultimate artistic vision?

Children naturally make space for these creative brain states, but as adults, we can cultivate them through practices like meditation, lowering our brainwave frequencies to tap into deeper layers of creativity. The more you meditate and play – in other words, the more you rest, and the more you embrace your dreamy inner child – the more likely you will be able to access the theta state, produce incredible things, and live a creative *and* successful life.

Benefits of stimulating theta brainwaves:

- Mind and body healing

- Boosted immune system

- Deep levels of relaxation

- Stress and anxiety reduction

- Intuition/subconscious connection

- Ability to program your unconscious mind

- High levels of creativity

Time to shine your creative superpowers to the world

Sifting through the pain (and making space for my heart) has become my mantra in life. It's helped me upscale my writing skills, quit my job, travel the world, write two books, and become a full-time writer, editor and writing coach. Now, I'm launching international retreats where I teach others to write from the heart. It's awakened a whole new creative reality for me. And I really can't explain to you how deeply satisfying it is to be committing to your soul work … while making money *and* making others happy with it.

Along the journey, each box I unpacked and each fear I faced revealed a little more of my true path. Meditation helped me hear the callings of my

HEARTWRITING: YOUR HEART ALWAYS HOLDS THE ANSWERS

heart so that I could hear my authentic voice – which is ultimately the source of my success. And with every step, the sound became clearer, light grew brighter, and my creative potential more palpable.

If you've always dreamed of becoming an artist, a dancer, a singer, a story writer, a musician – perhaps, like me, you need to sweep out those golden passages of creativity to make way for the writer or artist in you. It's not easy, but to shine a light on our shadows and step into our calling, we must first peer into the dark and clear away any lingering baggage. When the hallway of your heart is clear, and the old boxes are gone, you'll see a glimmering, golden path ahead: the passage of your creative dreams awaits.

HeartWriting Exercise
Theta Wave Writing Exercise: The Heart Connection

Access the theta brainwave state and tap into your uninhibited authentic voice and your innate creativity.

What You'll Need:

A quiet, comfortable space
A timer or gentle alarm
A notebook or your preferred writing tool
A comfortable seat or cushion
A small object (optional) to hold in your hand, like a smooth stone or a pen

Steps:

1. Set the Scene: Find a quiet place where you won't be disturbed for about 15-20 minutes. Sit comfortably, either in a chair or on a cushion, with your spine straight and your feet flat on the ground or legs crossed.

2. Begin with Breath: Close your eyes and take a few deep, calming breaths. Inhale slowly through your nose, allowing your belly to rise, and exhale through your mouth, letting go of any tension. Do this for a couple of minutes until you feel relaxed and centred.

3. Introduce a Mantra (Optional): If it helps, repeat a simple mantra or affirmation silently to yourself, such as 'I am open to creativity' or 'I write from my heart.' This can help guide your mind into a more focused, meditative state.

4. Focus on the Theta State: Allow yourself to relax even more deeply. Imagine your thoughts as clouds drifting across the sky – acknowledge them and let them pass. You're aiming to reach a state of deep relaxation, where your mind is quiet, yet alert. If you're holding an object, let your hand gently grip it, ready to release it if you start to drift off. The moment of 'almost sleep' is when you're likely dipping into the theta brainwave state.

5. Set Your Intention: Before you begin writing, set an intention: 'I will write from my heart.' This helps align your subconscious with your creative goals.

6. Free Write: Open your eyes, pick up your pen or start typing, and

begin to write whatever comes to mind. Don't censor yourself – just let the words flow. If you feel a bit drowsy or unfocused, that's perfect; it means you're likely in the theta state. Write for about 10-15 minutes.

7. Reflect: Once you've finished, take a moment to reflect on what you've written. Don't judge it – just notice the themes, emotions, and insights that emerged. This is your heart speaking. Notice how when you've shifted into a slower brainwave state, it allows you to hear your own voice, your dreams, your hurdles and your desires: your true voice that wants to come into the light.

8. Repeat Regularly: Try this exercise a few times a week. Do you notice how regular practice bring more 'aha' moments? Can you see how meditation can improve your heart connection? Over time, you'll find it easier to drop into the theta state, and you may notice that your writing becomes more authentic, inspired, and deeply connected to your inner self.

Optional Twist:

For those who enjoy a bit of a challenge, try setting an intention before your next nap or meditation session. Have a notebook nearby, and when you wake up, immediately write down whatever comes to mind. This can be a powerful way to capture that theta-state inspiration.

By regularly practising this exercise, you'll not only strengthen your ability to access the theta state but also deepen your connection to your heart's true voice, allowing your creativity to flow more naturally and authentically.

Want to learn more?

View the QR code to access a lesson on *The Magic And Science of the Creative Heart*. You'll also have the exclusive chance to download your free copy of my popular resource for writers: *The Heart Writing Journal*. Time to get writing and creating from the heart!

Chapter Eleven

Farmer of The Heart

Finding soul purpose and fulfillment in seeds of slowing down, stillness and tending to the soil of your own heart.

> With founder of Wayfinder Wellbeing, Kirsten Wojtowicz: an integrated wellness expert, biodynamic farmer and writer passionate about the everyday beauty and interconnectedness of life, who supports women to rest, restore and find their true soul-essence.

'For a seed to achieve its greatest expression, it must come completely undone. The shell cracks, its insides come out and everything changes. To someone who doesn't understand growth, it would look like complete destruction.'

Cynthia Occelli

Has life ever brought you to your knees? Those moments in time, forever changing your path of life. Those times you look skyward, asking 'why me', grappling with your purpose in life. I sure have.

I cradled my precious little bundle close to my heart. Willing her to breathe. But the stillness of death sat gently in the space. 12 years ago, I was an efficient multitasker, pushing through health issues and exhaustion to juggle long farm hours with multiple businesses. I yearned deeply for motherhood. It came as a flickering, joyful moment that unfolded into a harrowing journey through the deepest trenches of grief. Cracking the seed of my heart open, over and over, to an undivulged pain, which slowly transformed into wisdom and vast love from within.

This is my story of how my heart opened to life again through slowing down, embracing stillness and remembering the joy in growing potatoes. How I left a busy business, simplified my life and followed my soul's calling to become a 'farmer of the heart': a heart driven holistic practitioner who connects people back to themselves and the earth as a way of cultivating deep compassion and creating kind changes for themselves from within.

Have you ever been so efficient at 'doing' life that you've forgotten to tend to yourself, your soil, your soul?

In a world of technology, built upon seeing ourselves as separate from or superior to nature, society leans into a vortex of over consumption, extraction and productivity as we find ourselves busy 'doing' life. Most of us recognise we are busy and despite the stress and exhaustion we push on. To where? Perhaps fearful of our lack of purpose in life – if it all just stopped. Who would we be if we stopped doing?

The ancient practice of farming calls us back to 'be' in connection with nature, surrendering to the sacred soil of life, bowing with full breath to natural laws dictating rest and a return to Earth. There's wisdom in dirt. It took me many human experiences, dirt under my nails and hearty grit to understand the precious weaving between our being and the loam beneath our feet.

Mahatma Gandhi's words, *'to forget how to dig the earth and to tend the soil is to forget ourselves'* reminds us how easily our innate connection to earth can be forgotten when our minds and days are busy.

In my decades of biodynamic farm life, working in the paddocks barefoot helps me to remember. My soft underfoot sinks into fluffy chocolate soil, toes curling in delight as I negotiate undulating earth mounds. The morning is laced with soft dampness, sticks to my cheeks and squishes between my toes. My gaze follows the slope of the potato patch, lazily reaching to the golden yolk that has cracked on the horizon. Rows upon rows of potato bushes planted with the rusty blue tractor and its fat rolling tyres had stood skyward weeks ago. Now, wilting with a sagging, yellow trust.

The waft of sweet compost mingled with anticipation swirls up my nostrils as I plunge the pitch fork deep into the cushy loam. It freely fractures as I weigh back on the handle, exhuming the hope of a season. The soft depth of soil wrapping the potato in dark quietude, creates a space of humble growing. A place, I wonder if our hearts all know? The dirt crumbles away. Divine fleshy rubies are revealed. I pluck their naked, rosie bodies from the earth, rolling them through my fingertips brushing their delicate skins. I burrow again, gifted seven full tubers. I lift up the front of my flannel shirt, thread bare with love, cradling my waxy babies. My heart is full. Fresh dug potatoes for dinner. Here, in this simple moment, I remember my place in all things. The soil holds us all, even in dark times, whispering heart truths and offering abundance if only we are still enough to listen.

Just like the potato patch, there are many delightful treasures waiting to be unearthed in all of us, if given a quiet space to rest and grow.

Wendell Berry writes '*a sustainable agriculture is one which depletes neither the people nor the land*'.

The method of biodynamic farming, honours rested ground. Consciously giving back to the soil with green crops and rotations, to nourish and build living soil while gentle cultivation oxygenates the earth. Allowing the farm, a deep exhalation. A rest from production and extraction.

I zealously applied these beautiful concepts to the farm but neglected to nourish myself in the same way. At my lowest point – despite living the idyllic wholesome farm life and my knowledge of natural medicine – *I was an empty husk.*

At that time, my farming reality was long hours, labour intensive work and juggling the weekly commitment of supplying hundreds of families with fresh produce each week. Season after season, the cycle of perpetual harvest and doing more rolled on. Extraction and depletion amplified by the loss of my baby girl, the defeat of endless miscarriages, an autoimmune condition and heart wrenching family rifts was a cycle that would usher in the death of all I thought I was. Buried deeply in an unknown darkness, I paused my business of 18 years and sunk into my body that had no more capacity for 'doing'. My soul, my soil was aching to be nourished.

Alexandra Crosswell Ph.D. explains here, I needed a deep rest.

'Deep rest isn't just a brief moment of relaxation; it's a profound psychophysiological state that rejuvenates both the mind and the body. Often the stress of daily life leads to many people experiencing persistent dominance of their sympathetic nervous system, which makes it difficult to experience the benefits of deep rest except during the deepest stages of sleep'.

I had accumulated years of overwork and trauma but lacked tools to recalibrate my nervous system. To find balance within. Deep rest was my first step on the path back.

When was the last time you sunk deep into your bones and exhaled fully?

Paused rather than pushed? If you're in a space like I was, resting may sound crazy or not an option. But the possibilities and healing when your soul is given space to pause and consciously restore are life-changing.

Our society cultivates a work culture reinforcing hard work earns rest. But the soil suggests an alternate option; well rested soil produces abundant and healthy crops, the most hearty of potatoes. Imagine being so deeply rested you showed up in the world with your whole heart, full of purpose and clarity.

So, what does one do if they are not doing?

Conscious rest takes the form of self-care, self-kindness and regular practices that connect you back to yourself and your true nature.

For me, this looked like wandering from the farm to a yoga class, with a grubby blue mat, active wear airing holes from barbed wire fences and an inability to touch my toes. I was the person in the back row that meditated with one eye open.

Sitting on my mat, in this new space, my heart cracked open. Yoga was not what I thought it was. There was an unfurling of kindness for myself, sinking tiny fuzzy roots of breath into the darkest edges of my soul. Into the still void, the dirt of me, the divinity that has always held me. Yoga practice introduced my body to new shapes and stretches, connecting with breath, stillness and a community of warm hugs and belly laughs that gave space for new shoots of my being to reach upward.

Connecting quietly with my heart became something I craved and a simple ritual that I could do at home. Perched on my cushion under the peaceful guard of two silver birches, I would feel into the corners of my body with breath. Sitting on the verandah, journal in lap, the spice of a warm chai hitting my insides as I watched flocks of white fluff wander the sky or dappled light playing through the leaves. The voice of treasured meditation teacher Mark Pheely lolling in the distance – 'how is your heart today?'

With consistent meditation practice, I experienced the well-researched benefits of stress and anxiety reduction, better sleep, less pain, enhanced self-awareness and greater compassion, simply by allowing myself to be.

I am still humbled by the transformation that occurred, not only mentally, but to my entire being, A significant amount of body weight fell away with kindness, autoimmune issues dissolved, sound sleep became cherished medicine and my body moved with ease and a vital strength that hummed with the simple joy of being alive. The even greater gift was having space to write the poems I'd been crafting in my heart through all my experiences and to share my words with others.

The sweet and powerful surrender found in the daily ritual of stillness laced my being with a deep woven trust in nature and our divine place within its intelligence.

An understanding that we, like much of the Earth, are in constant cycles of growth and decay. And in those vulnerable and painful moments when we find ourselves in the darkness, life returns us to the depths of the soil; the ability to sit quietly, feel into all of it with breath, and trust that cosmic forces are pulling us gently upward takes immense courage.

Seeds planted in the hearts of well rested souls hold a wisdom of rooted knowing, trusting the process of transformation and welcoming the full expression of self to heal, flourish and live well.

And by the way, there is a bounty of steaming, pop-skinned goodness in my bowl right now. Buttery puddles and soft, welcoming potatoes that squish open as I bear down with the fork. The first mouthful speaks a hearty depth of soul knowing. The humble potato holds a universe of wisdom within and reminds me of all life. I am grateful to be given this simple moment to devour with absolute delight.

> **EXERCISE: Cup of Tea With Your Heart Stillness Practice**
>
> 1. Brew your favourite cup of tea. Stir with quiet intention.
> 2. Set yourself up comfortably in a quiet space with a chair or a

cushion on the ground.

3. Hold your cup of tea to your heart and gently close your eyes or hold a soft gaze.

4. Take a few deep breaths. Allow yourself to settle. Perhaps notice noises coming and going, the warmth of your tea near your heart, the smell of your brew touching your nostrils, notice where your body connects and is being held by the earth.

5. Focus on breath. Inhale slowly, resting your focus on the pause at the end of the breath. Exhale slowly through your mouth, letting go of tension. At the end of each inhale hold the pause a little longer, feeling the space of the pause expanding within your body. Not forced. Not holding. Just falling into the softness of breath, witnessing the gentle stillness growing within you with each breath. Continue for a few minutes, feeling yourself relax.

6. Ask yourself: How does your heart feel today? Witness the emotions and thoughts arising. Happy, sad, tired, joyful – welcome them all, just allowing your heart to be heard.

7. Gently open your eyes & sip your tea in a moment of self-reflection.

8. Option to journal here, writing out whatever arises, without judgment. Allowing your heart to speak on paper.

9. Craft a ritual 3 times a week. Replacing 'routine' with 'ritual' can make a cup of tea feel most sacred. Meeting with your heart through meditation is a beautiful practice that cultivates a deeper connection to inner self.

References and quotes

- Cynthia Occelli Quote, Author & Coach https://www.cynthiaoccelli.com

- Pathhak H, 2020 **Mahatma Ghandi's Vision of Agriculture** pg 86 https://icar.org.in/sites/default/files/2022-06/Gandhi-Ji-Book-16-10-2020-m.pdf

- Wendell Berry Quote//Farmers Footprint Australia 2024, https://farmersfootprint.org.au/reconnect-a-farmer-health-and-wellbeing-retreat/

- Alexandra Crosswell, 2024 **The Science of Deep rest: A Gateway to Sustained Wellness,** Psychology Today

- https://www.psychologytoday.com/au/blog/the-compassionate-brain/202404/the-science-of-deep-rest-a-gateway-to-sustained-wellness

- Mark Pheely Quote Yoga & Meditation Teacher https://www.markpheely.com

Chapter Twelve

A Lost and Found

Re-discovering yourself and reigniting your inner sparkle.

> It's never too late! A journey of self-exploration and rediscovering your true self through creative pursuits, radiating your inner light. A perspective by Tracey Summerfield-Owers.

Do you wake up some mornings feeling empty, weighed down by a heaviness in your heart – the loss of who you are? Are you struggling to reconnect with your inner light, your sparkle? This sensation of disconnection can be deeply unsettling, leaving you to question the essence of your being. In today's fast-paced world, it's easy to lose sight of ourselves amid the demands and expectations placed upon us as mothers, partners, employees or employers, daughters to ageing parents, aunties, sisters, and supportive friends to many.

For years, I felt trapped by the relentless pace of life, disconnected from my true self, and questioning my purpose. Major life events, such as marrying at 21, realising my mistake just three months later, and then divorcing 12 months later made me feel like a failure. I remarried and inherited a stepfamily, which brought its challenges. As the children from our marriage grew independent, we looked forward to being *'empty nesters'*. This was not to be, as my partner's eldest daughter lost custody of her children due to her drug addiction. We agreed to care for her 4-year-old daughter, despite her father being able but unwilling to take responsibility.

Taking on a child with trauma was overwhelming, and we felt unprepared and unsupported. I had a fulfilling career in university administration, but suddenly I was back to managing school drop-offs and pickups, sorting out lunches, responsible for playdates, and sporting activities. At 52, I also felt I was having to put my life and career on hold again, while caring for my ageing parents.

I eventually reached a point of burnout from the relentless challenges of my caregiving roles. I felt defeated, losing touch with myself as I neglected to prioritise my own needs and nurture the passion within me. The idea of saying '*no*' never crossed my mind; I felt guilty at the thought of putting myself first. As a people pleaser, I often said '*yes*' when I wanted to say '*no*', which deepened my sense of disconnection. In the process, I overlooked vital practices like self-care and reflection. This lack of introspection only intensified my feelings of sadness.

Listen to the whispers of your heart when they speak to you

There were many times my heart tried to talk to me and let me know I wanted or needed more from life, but I ignored it for so long, as I felt my place was to care for my family.

My 'aha moment' came when I realised that this journey back to myself is not about abandoning responsibilities, but about *finding a balance that nurtured my Soul and ignited my Spirit within*. I was drawn to information and books on self-discovery and the power of a positive mindset and the inner spirit. How important gratitude is in our daily life. I asked myself – *'What is Soul Loss?'*

Does the above resonate with you? You are not alone. Read further to learn how I was able to pause, rest, and start my journey to self-discovery. **It is never too late!**

Concept of Soul

The concept of the *'Soul'* refers to the deepest part of ourselves, the essence that thinks, feels, and drives our actions. It is our spiritual dimension, distinct from the physical aspects of our lives. The Soul represents our core identity and intrinsic light, which guides and inspires us. When the light dims, it can feel as though a vital part of us has been lost, making it difficult to experience true fulfilment.

Understanding Soul Loss

'Soul Loss' is a term that describes the sensation of losing access to this vital core of your being. It doesn't necessarily mean a literal loss but rather a disconnection from your inner self, your spirit. You might have a successful career, a loving partner, and beautiful children – an outwardly fulfilling life. Friends enjoy your company, and you appear to have everything one could wish for. Yet, despite these external successes, you may find yourself grappling with a profound sense of unhappiness and a heavy heart. This disparity between external achievements and internal fulfilment can be unsettling. It's natural to question: *'Why am I feeling this way?' 'How can I rekindle my inner sparkle?'*

My journey to rediscovery started after attending a work-related personal development mindful workshop, where part of the introduction to the day was a ten-minute guided meditation, pausing and resting to listen to my inner voice, to be in the present moment. These ten minutes seemed much longer and at the end of the meditation, I was like WOW I need this to be part of my daily schedule.

There were other takeaways from the day that kicked started my intentions to continue seeking other workshops and activities that would ultimately guide me in finding who I was and what soothed my Soul, and I discuss my favourites down below.

You can find your sparkle again: Embrace your self-discovery journey

Self-discovery can be very powerful and often involves exploring various aspects of our identity. Self-discovery is a lifelong journey. There are times when setting out to reconnect to your inner glow can feel like an elusive dance. Stay strong and true to yourself once you start your journey. Psychology suggests that this journey offers personal growth and happiness.

Take time to reflect on your values, passions, and interests

Look in the mirror and tell yourself you are awesome – look at all the things you have achieved and the hardships you have overcome to be where you are right now. You are strong and resilient and deserve to love yourself wholeheartedly and are deserving of love from all the special people in your life.

It is OK to take time out for YOU!

Don't allow the self-chatter of *'It's selfish of me to want to do activities that are just for me'*. No, it is not! Time out for you is crucial for you to be your authentic self. The off spin from this is that you will also be a role model for those around you. When our hearts sing our inner sparkle flows out and people around us enjoy basking in your light. Take intentional steps to reconnect with what brings you joy and fulfilment. Reflecting on what are your values, and passions that you may have stopped or wanted to try but never got around to it.

For me this understanding and acceptance marked a significant shift in how I approached my life and well-being. A realisation that I was important and self-love was what I needed to bring back my true self.

The following are a few tips to get started on your self-discovery journey. You will carve out your own pathway and will add things to the list that are right for you.

Tips to reignite and shine your inner light

Reflection: Ask yourself the following questions and write down your responses.

I like to review my response down the track and check in with myself to see what I have changed and what is different for me now. Make sure to add the date.

What are my values? Am I asking myself to do things that are against my personal beliefs and values?

What are my achievements to date? You will be surprised by the number of great things you have achieved that you may have forgotten about or that you devalue but are so important for where you are in your life at that moment.

What things am I doing that do not bring me joy that I can discard or do differently?

What activities or experiences bring me joy? For me, this was to reignite my passion for creating with clay and paint. I enrolled in art classes. The amazing thing about doing this was I had forgotten how much pleasure working with clay and painting gave me. The bonus was the new friendships I made and connecting with like-minded women.

Dream big

Envision what you would do if you had a magic wand. Allow yourself to dream without limits. For me, there are a few things: one is to create an art studio where I can immerse myself in ceramics and painting, and another is to travel and experience different cultures. Just thinking about this dream inspires me and energises me to pursue it. Dreams are not constant and will change as we are forever evolving as we achieve goals and life takes us in different directions.

Practice gratitude

Our brains are naturally inclined toward negativity, a remnant of our evolutionary past when constant alertness was necessary for survival. However, we can shift this bias toward positivity by consciously reflecting on what we are grateful for. As noted by Kendra Cherry, MSEd, on VeryWellMind,

'Research has shown that negative bias can have a wide variety of effects on how people think, respond, and feel.'

To counteract negativity, try a daily gratitude exercise. Keep a journal by your bedside and write down three things you're grateful for each morning. This simple practice can shift your mindset and foster a more positive outlook on life.

Practice mindfulness

John Kabat-Zinn (1994), one of the most popular Western writers on this topic and creator of the Mindfulness-Based Stress Reduction program (MBSR), defines mindfulness as *'the awareness that arises through paying attention, on purpose, in the present moment, non-judgmentally.'*

Mindfulness involves being fully present and aware of where you are and what you're doing without being overwhelmed by your surroundings. It helps ground you in the present moment and can significantly improve your sense of connection and well-being. Practising mindfulness allows you to reset your mind. It takes self-awareness but the benefits are worth the persistence of practice.

Some examples of that worked for me.

Writing down a to-do list is also useful to clear your mind and allows you to focus on one task at a time.

Taking breaks. During work hours, take time for your breaks. A walk around the block just to reset. For me this is invaluable. I was in an admin job where I sat all day, answering phones, emails, and attending meetings and consultations with students. I would eat lunch at my desk. This was a habit that I changed by practising mindfulness and taking my lunch away from my desk. Being mindful, taking a break, and enjoying your lunch, walk, or whatever resets your mind. Some studies indicate taking a walk during the day also increases your productivity.

Meditation

Meditation involves directing our attention to the subtle, often overlooked aspects of our experience. It emphasises qualities such as softness, tenderness, and kindness, particularly towards ourselves. The practice aims to reconnect with and restore the various dimensions of our being – dimensions that were never truly lost, but may have been obscured or neglected. Essentially, meditation helps us reawaken and realign with our inherent, complete nature.

Guided meditation websites that offer free trial guided meditation resources:

1. Insight Timer – Offers a wide variety of free guided meditations, including those led by experienced teachers.

2. Headspace – Provides a selection of free guided meditations, including introductory sessions for beginners.

3. Calm – Features a range of free guided meditations and mindfulness exercises.

4. Smiling Mind – Provides free guided meditations and mindfulness programs, especially geared towards different age groups.

5. My Meditation – Offers a collection of free guided meditation

recordings and resources.

These resources can help you explore different styles of meditation and find what works best for you.

Prioritise self-care

Putting yourself first is not selfish but essential for maintaining balance and well-being. Pause before saying yes to new commitments, and allow yourself the space to rest and reflect. Engage in activities that bring you joy and fulfilment, and be open to spontaneity.

The importance of self-care cannot be emphasised enough. It encompasses all that has been written above.

Here are some self-care tips to help you maintain your well-being and balance:

1. **Prioritise Sleep**: Aim for 7-9 hours of quality sleep each night. Establish a regular sleep routine and create a restful environment.

2. **Eat Nutritious Foods**: Incorporate a balanced diet rich in fruits, vegetables, whole grains, and lean proteins to nourish your body.

3. **Exercise Regularly**: Engage in physical activity you enjoy, such as walking, yoga, or dancing, to boost your mood and energy levels.

4. **Practice Mindfulness and Meditation**: Spend a few minutes each day practising mindfulness or meditation to reduce stress and enhance mental clarity.

5. **Set Boundaries**: Learn to say no when necessary and set limits to

avoid overcommitting yourself.

6. **Pause and rest**: Give yourself regular breaks throughout the day to relax and recharge, whether it's a short walk, a deep breathing exercise, or simply sitting quietly.

7. **Connect with Loved Ones**: Spend time with family and friends who support and uplift you, and seek out meaningful social interactions.

8. **Seek Professional Help**: If you're feeling overwhelmed, don't hesitate to reach out to a psychologist or counsellor for support.

9. **Practice Gratitude**: Take a moment each day to reflect on what you're grateful for, which can help shift your focus to positive aspects of life.

10. **Disconnect from Technology**: Take time to unplug from digital devices and social media to reduce stress and improve focus.

11. **Spontaneity of life.** Be spontaneous, and do things on the spur of the moment. Not everything needs to be planned.

12. **Do things you love, or always wanted to try**. Make time for activities you love, whether it's reading, painting, gardening, listening to music, or playing an instrument.

Incorporating some or all of these self-care practices into your life can help you maintain balance, reduce stress, and nurture overall well-being and personal growth.

Explore personal growth

Enrol in workshops, read self-help books and seek resources that resonate with you. These tools can offer new perspectives and strategies for personal growth. Accept that you will continually change and disappointments and sadness are part of life. Reflect on these experiences without punishing yourself. Instead, recognise the growth that comes from overcoming challenges and cherish the positive memories and successes.

Motivational quotes

I enjoy following motivational and positive quotes on Facebook. While not every quote resonates, many of them inspire me to stay true to my heart and authentic self.

> *'Your Mind is a Powerful thing. When you fill it with positive thoughts, your life will begin to change.'*
>
> Power of Positivity (Facebook)

Life's better with an inner sparkle

After what feels like a lifetime of doing things for others, I now explore my creative nature and dabble in ceramics, mosaics, and mixed media art. I even consider myself an evolving artist as my studio is nearing its completion. I listen to music, turn the volume up loud, and dance. I am not afraid to be spontaneous and will do things on the spur of the moment. I have learned the importance of putting myself first and saying no to things that do not serve my authentic self with meaningful purpose.

Practising self-care and self-love has become essential for me, especially after my husband's passing following a brief battle with cancer. It has helped me understand myself better and identify what I need to heal from the loss of someone I deeply loved and who played such a significant role in my life for many years.

Self-discovery is a lifelong undertaking that calls for patience, self-compassion, and focus. By reconnecting with your core values and nurturing your soul, you'll not only revive your inner light but also strengthen your connections with others. Trust that every step you take brings you closer to a more vibrant and authentic version of yourself. Embrace this process of rediscovery and let yourself shine brightly once again.

Chapter Thirteen

Journey to Your True Authentic Self

To truly understand who you are, you must first understand who you are not.

> With Kia Miller, internationally renowned yoga and spiritual teacher, lover of life and founder of Radiant Body Yoga.

Embarking on the journey to your true authentic self, is not a quest for something new, but a return to who you have always been. It begins with a simple yet profound question:

What do you truly desire?

This is not just a superficial wish but a deep, heartfelt longing that reflects the essence of your being.

Alongside this, consider the barriers that seem to hold you back – the challenges that appear insurmountable. These challenges are not mere obstacles; they are the very catalysts that, when faced with courage and curiosity, guide you closer to your true self. This chapter invites you to explore these questions, delve into the unseen forces that shape your life, and embrace the journey of self-discovery with an open heart.

To begin, take a moment now to ask yourself ... *What is my deepest desire? What is that wild, uncontainable aspiration that makes my heart race?* Now, consider this – *what is my greatest challenge*? What is the one thing that seems to stand between me and the life I know I am meant to live?

These are not just casual questions.

Most of us are living to just a fraction of what we are capable of. You might find yourself repeatedly facing the same challenges, getting stuck in the same sort of situations and attracting similar types of relationships? I have been there too. I used to attract the wrong kind of relationships, as my desire for love and approval outweighed my common sense. When I met my husband, I could not see the potential, I wrote him off as 'a player, too charming and handsome' to be real, where actually he is one of the most genuine loving people I know. It was two of my girlfriends who said to me *'What about Tommy? We love Tommy for you.'* They opened my eyes to something I could not see as I was used to a different frequency match, one that was often a reflection of my insecurities and limitations.

What I have learned over the years is that if you are not working with conscious desires, like the desire for a healthy loving relationship, then you will be at the mercy of your unconscious desires. For me, this was the unconscious desire for love and approval that coloured all of my interactions.

The Yoga Tradition teaches that the solution to all problems begins with the individual, and that within each individual lies infinite potential. That means within me, and of course *within you!* To reach this reservoir of inner potential you have to be prepared to tune in to your innermost desires, and to unpack your unconscious beliefs that are holding you back.

The simple but important questions above are keys to help awaken within you a new level of authenticity. Being willing to stand in the discomfort of claiming what you truly desire, of learning to confidently self-reflect and self-correct. This journey requires courage, curiosity, and a willingness to step out of the old way of being and embrace the unknown. Who are you without the limitations of the past?

We attract what we believe and what we are

Life, at its core, is vibrational. Our unconscious beliefs are the lens through which we see the world. They shape how we interpret events, interact with others and respond to life's challenges, and they actually emit vibrations that attract corresponding or similar experiences into our lives.

What does this mean?

It means that what you put out into the world, comes back to you. For example, when we don't feel good enough, lovable or worthy we attract people into our lives that don't see our beauty and goodness. The great news is, when you understand the way this works, change is possible. To change your life, you must first change the frequency you vibrate at, e.g. how you see and feel about yourself and your life right now.

In my own life, I found one of the most important aspects of the journey to the authentic self, was to *'open to Grace'*. A process you learn through yoga, of becoming aware of and recognising the unseen support and magic that permeates every aspect of life. Recognising that you are not alone, that there is a divine intelligence guiding you.

Accessing this support requires more than just intellectual understanding; it requires the application of specific tools and techniques that help you elevate your vibrational state such as practices that move your energy, release emotional stuckness, and open you to experience a deeper connection to yourself.

I remember a powerful navel kriya (set of exercises) that challenged me to reach my edge. In the relaxation right after the core exercises, I had a profound experience of recognising my 'self' I could feel myself as though for the first time. I could see how many masks I had been wearing and presenting to the world that were not me, but what I thought others wanted to see. This profound moment literally changed me forever. In retrospect, this was a combination of positive self-effort in the kriya, and then surrender as I relaxed and allowed a new experience in. As I have developed in my practice, I realise how important it is to be able to move through stuckness, dissolve old masks, and experience new vibrational states that fill me with the trust and confidence to be more authentic in all of my interactions.

When you shift your vibrational state, it allows you to perceive all your challenges from a different perspective, transforming obstacles into opportunities for growth.

Become like a mystic

What have you always dreamed of being or doing?

People dream of becoming teachers, pilots, artists, coaches, actors, pop stars or running their own freedom business. I had many dreams, and many lives in this one, yet, when I stepped on the path of yoga, I knew that this was my dream, to teach, to take people through transformative experiences, to walk in the footprints of mystics.

I have always been fascinated by mystics – those rare individuals who march to the beat of their own drum, who seem to have access to a deeper, more profound understanding of life. I have encountered mystics in many shapes and forms, often in the most unlikely of places, and each one has entered my life bearing gifts of wisdom and insight. If I had to name one primary desire in my own life now, this definition of a mystic that I paraphrased from a quote from the Oxford languages dictionary, is exactly it: *'A mystic is a person who seeks by contemplation and self-surrender to obtain unity with or absorption into the absolute.'*

The essence of the mystic's journey is the same journey we must all undertake if we are to access our authentic selves. It is a journey that begins with contemplation – a deep, honest inquiry into who we truly are, beneath the layers of social conditioning and egoic identity.

This contemplation often reveals uncomfortable truths about the ways in which we have allowed fear, resistance, and doubt to dictate our lives. But it also reveals something far more profound: the presence of Grace, an *unseen force* that is always available to us, guiding us to grow and thrive.

For many years I thought that to become fully awakened to my inner power, my authentic self was not possible in this life. I believed it was only for the special few who possessed something I lacked. I felt inadequate and lacked confidence in myself.

But deep down, in the quiet recesses of my heart, I knew I was capable of so much more. I knew that pursuing a connection with the magical and mystical aspects of existence, was the thing that would influence my life the most.

I have found that the best tools to access these mystical aspects are yoga, in particular Kundalini Yoga, mantra and meditation.

You may relate when I say however, that for years I felt like I was merely playing the role of meditating as I did not know how to fully immerse myself in the experience. I meditated because I was told it would work by teachers I trusted. I would sit and go through the motions, just to get through it and be able to tell myself that I had done the task I set out to do. I tried so many different kinds of meditations and I kept at it. *'Keep trying, consistently, over time you will progress.'* This is what my teachers said.

One day it changed and suddenly everything shifted for me.

It came to me as I sat in meditation. I was sitting on the edge of absorption, sensing my inner lethargy, feeling like I was playing the role of meditating, then I caught the identity who was pretending and switched to simply being aware and surrendering to the experience of energy in my body, feeling it fullness, its resonance, how safe and pleasant it was, like being submerged in a luminous ball of light that buzzed and reverberated. I was being wrapped in an inner blanket, so cosy and soft. I was vaguely aware of the other me, the personality on stand-by waiting to comment on my experience, but chose again to feel the exquisite pulse within that grew as I focussed on it. *This is it. This is me. This is God. This is now.*

I felt my heart respond to the experience with a rush of gratitude, love, and understanding. It was as if I had tapped into a wellspring of divine essence, a source of infinite love and wisdom that had always been within me, waiting to be acknowledged.

This experience was an instant and profound reminder, that the journey to our authentic selves is not about becoming something we are not; it is about remembering who we have always been. Shedding the layers of temporary identification – the roles, labels, and beliefs that we have accumulated over the years – and allowing a merger with something bigger than ourselves. The infinite source of love and wisdom that permeates everything.

To fully understand who we are, we must first understand who we are not

The paradox of life is that in order to fully understand who we are, we must first understand who we are not. We must identify the layers of egoic identity that keep us stuck in smallness and fear, and we must be willing to let them go. This is not an easy process, but it is a necessary one if we are to access our authentic selves and live the life that we dream of.

As a child, I intuitively felt one with the Divine. I felt held, seen, and deeply connected to a mysterious presence that watched over me. I spoke to this presence often, especially when I was alone or with animals or loved ones. Even in my darkest moments, I could sense this subtle presence, a gentle reminder that I was never truly alone. But as I grew older, I began to drift away from this connection. I experienced long periods of heaviness, like a dark cloud that suffocated me, drained my spirit and took away any belief that there was something more out there. Something bigger to connect to, than myself. You personally may know this as Source, God, Spirit, or the Universe.

It took many years of searching, of trying on different identities and philosophies, before I finally understood that the presence I felt as a child was not something external to me. It was the essence of who I am. It is the essence of who we all are. And it is always available to us, no matter how lost or disconnected we may feel.

You see, when we drift away from the higher frequencies of love, grace, and resonance, life becomes a series of painful and disorienting experiences. The absence of these guiding forces often manifests as a lack of presence, where we feel disconnected from ourselves and the world around us. It is in this disconnection that we fall prey to anxiety, depression, or self-destructive behaviours as we search for ways to fill the void. Like vibration attracts like vibration, depression and discontentment attract and create more depression and discontentment, and we can get caught in what feels like a downward spiral of darkness, regret and self-blame. These are the moments we need to create a vibrational shift.

Raising your frequency using yoga

One of the most powerful tools for raising your frequency is the practice of yoga. In this context, I mean yoga that includes movement, breathwork, kriyas (specific sequences to liberate energy), mantra and meditation. Yoga is a journey from the gross to the subtle – stuck, bound and limited, to freedom and unlimited possibilities. A process of first getting into the body, then opening it up to receive – whether that be nutrition, love, or new possibilities. As you activate your vital life force through yoga, you begin to tap into your personal power, and from there, the deeper healing begins.

Yoga teaches you to harness our inner energy, to move through blocks, and to create a purpose-driven, meaningful life. But yoga is not just a physical practice; it is a spiritual journey. It is a path that leads us back to our true nature, to the divine essence that resides within us all.

As you deepen your practice, you will find that the lines between the physical and the mystical begin to blur. You will start to see the world with new eyes and an open heart, and you will begin to experience the magic and mystery of life in ways you never thought possible.

This reflects a vibrational shift, where your energy has reached a new frequency, and the mystical elements of life become available. You become aware of synchronicities, and you attract and magnetise new opportunities into your life.

The journey to your authentic self is a journey of love

The journey of accessing your true authentic self requires deep, radical personal honesty. Are you willing to drop your masks and follow the call that comes from deep within? This journey requires tools, courage, and commitment. It is messy and challenging, yet it is also filled with immense beauty, joy, and love that ultimately lead to the greatest love affair of all – the love affair with the Divine essence within you.

As you embark on this journey, I encourage you to become aware of where you are caught in fear and resistance. Fear indicates an opportunity to move into the unknown, to birth something new. Resistance indicates what you are holding on to that is, in turn, holding you back.

One of the key teachings in yoga is that we must learn to surrender – surrender our ego, our fears, and our need for control. This surrender is not a sign of weakness but a profound act of courage. It is a recognition that there is a greater force at work in our lives, a force that is guiding us toward our highest potential. When we surrender, we create space for this force to enter and work its magic. We open ourselves up to the infinite possibilities that exist beyond the limitations of our mind.

This is a journey of awakening.

It is a process of peeling back the layers of mistaken identity to reveal the radiant, powerful being that you truly are. It is a journey that requires patience, persistence, and a deep trust in the process. As you continue to walk this path, you will notice subtle shifts in your life. You will feel more aligned, more connected, and more in tune with the natural flow of the universe.

The beauty of this journey is that it is never truly over. There is always more to discover, more to learn, and more to experience. Each moment is an opportunity to deepen your connection with your authentic self and with the divine essence that resides within you. The more you align with this essence, the more you will experience the magic, wonder, and joy that life has to offer.

In the end, the journey to your authentic self is a journey of love.

A love that transcends all boundaries. A love that is unconditional and eternal. It is a love that begins with yourself and extends to all beings. As you access this love, you will find that your life begins to unfold in ways that are beyond your wildest dreams. You will attract the people, opportunities, and experiences that are in perfect resonance with your true self. You will live a life of purpose, passion, and profound fulfilment.

EXERCISE 1:

I invite you now to take the first step on this journey.

Take a deep breath, close your eyes, and listen to your quiet voice within.

What is your next step toward acknowledging and representing your authentic self?

What's your first answer?

What frequency does this authentic Self vibrate at? What would you be feeling when you have reached this place?

If you are not yet embodying this frequency. Embark on an upgrade through yogic, breath or meditation practices. This will help you to raise your frequency so that you can feel this authenticity in every cell of your body.

Repeat the process as necessary.

In the process, trust in yourself, and trust in the divine intelligence that is guiding you every step of the way. Quantum leaps come when you embrace the unknown, rise up to turn challenges into opportunities, and embody the truth of who you are – *beautiful, radiant, and precious.*

This is your journey and opportunity to shine. So, go forth with courage, grace, and love, and remember to take pauses in the moments when challenged, where you reunite with your inner BE-ing.

EXERCISE 2:

If you would like to try out some powerful tools for raising your frequency and support you on the path to fully embodying your authentic self – yoga, breathwork, kriyas (specific sequences to liberate energy), mantra and meditation – I invite you to join me on this transformative journey in our free Radiant Body Yoga community, where you'll connect with thousands of like-minded souls committed to love and living extraordinary lives.

WORTHY AND WELL

Stories about health, mental health, wellness and self-worth, how they all link together and what you can do for yourself.

Chapter Fourteen

Pain to Purpose

How unexpressed emotional pain impacts on the physical body, mental and emotional health, how to release it and how to prevent recurrences of it.

An Integrative Holistic Approach to Health and Wellbeing with Dr Vasambal Manikkam: Trauma Informed Nutritional Food Science Expert, Yoga Devotee and Accredited Holistic Health Promotion Practitioner Working With Evidence-Based Healing Modalities.

'It is during our darkest moments that we must focus to see the light.'

Buddha

If you experience chronic physical body pains, mental health issues, emotional traumas and/or stress, you are not alone.

According to the U.S. Centre for Disease Control and Prevention (CDC), an estimated 20.9% of the population in 2021 (more than 51.6 million Americans) suffered from chronic pain[1]. And 70% of all chronic pain sufferers are women[2].

But, what is chronic pain? Yale Medicine defines chronic pain as *'discomfort that persists or progresses over a long period of time. It might be 'on' and 'off', or it might be continuous. Chronic pain may last for months or even years. Some major categories of chronic pain include musculoskeletal pain, abdominal or pelvic pain, and headaches and migraines*[2]*.'*

Many researchers are *'starting to attribute some of this difference to the layered levels of stress a woman experiences. Women are more likely than men to report experiencing severe stress (28 percent compared to 20 percent of men), likely due to the unique acute and chronic stressful circumstances in the lives of women*[2]*.'*

From my personal experience, I, one hundred percent, firmly believe this to be true. I am the primary witness that unexpressed emotional pain and stress cause chronic physical pain and that when you are not able to process your traumas, stress, and emotions right away, they end up being stored in your body, at the deepest cellular level. And guess what? They actually accumulate and grow.

I know through intense studies and research that our physical body, an extremely intelligent instrument, is speaking with us every single fraction of a second, and that emotional pain can be stored within our cells, tissues and organs. As an expert in food, nutrition, gut-brain axis, non-communicable diseases (NCDs), appetite-regulatory hormones and women's health, I confirm this scientifically. This knowledge, however, didn't stop me from falling into the same behaviours so many of my clients seek my help for today.

You see … I have swallowed decades of suppressed emotions – anger, distress, sadness, frustrations, etc. that were *never* allowed to be expressed, from a very young age. Added with my long-term stress and unresolved traumas, they all became my *'silent killer'* to my healthy cells that wreaked havoc onto my physical body and overall health, until I delved deeper, understood what was happening, and gave myself permission to turn it all around.

Here is my story of resounding pain, depression and darkness, to peace, prosperity, purpose and illuminating bright light ...

For many years, despite having LEARNED, LAUGHED, SMILED, TRAVELLED, ADVENTURED and LIVED A LOT along my journey thus far, I have experienced significant levels of emotional pain and darkness in my life to the point where I once was suicidal and tried unsuccessfully to commit suicide. I have lived through an unplanned devastating break-up, negative criticisms, rejections, unfair dismissals and dismissed bullying. All these accumulated into enormous amounts of intolerable stresses, heart ache, and the storage of negative emotions, such as resentment, anger, rage, sadness, grievances, confusion, overwhelm, disappointment, etc.

These became fully expressed within my entire body in the form of unexplained extreme body pains, which I defined as *'A HAMMER HITTING ME DEEP INSIDE!'* Extreme migraines, neck, shoulder, spinal and debilitating menstrual pains. The trapped emotions also led to my appetite loss, emotional eating, and the overindulgence of food as coping mechanisms, on top of poor sleep quality, impacting severely on my central nervous system.

Despite all of this, and in fact because of all this, I held my head up high, survived, rose up, reached for the sky, and I am now able to support others on a similar journey. It was not an easy road as ABCD, but my healing journey took a lot of learning and unlearning that drove me towards my new roadmap of conscious healthy eating, pain alleviation, emotional cleansing, spirituality, self-care, self-acceptance, forgiveness, loving and finding myself, and setting boundaries to protect my innocent and sensitive light. This is when and where I discovered that everything I was experiencing was strongly interconnected.

My unique childhood and growth development phase

Growing up as a child on the serene and peaceful island of Mauritius, my childhood seemed normal and beautiful. I played marbles, hide and seek, hopscotch (*la marelle*), kite flying, etc. I loved being outdoors in nature, in the sun, climbing big lemon trees, and getting my hands dirty in the soil. I was surrounded by dogs, cats, chicken, roosters, and more tropical fruit trees (mangoes, papaya, jackfruit, etc.). It was my safe space. I adored the simple living style. I still do. In my locality, I was known for my petite figure, softness, kindness, quietness, innocence, obedience, my consideration for others, and my infectious smile. I was the *'good girl'*. Customers loved me, especially the ways I wrapped gifts and parcels. *'It was done with love. It was clean and neat. It was genuine service,'* said the customers.

Despite the serenity and the rich memories of feeling content, it was a patriarchal society. Women never questioned their place and self-worth. Mental and emotional health were taboo and never spoken of and self-esteem was never a theme. Life was all about working and studying hard, achievements, discipline and strictness. Saying YES was respectful to my Elders, and there was absolutely no questioning this. There was a certain way that things needed to be done, and do it PERFECTLY, or else I was NO GOOD. I always had to be a *'good'* and happy girl, and kind and gentle to others. Crying and expressing myself, my pains and emotions were not allowed. I'd get told off for these, as they were seen as weaknesses in a male-driven society. So, I developed a tough skin on the outside wrapped with a thin layer of innocence, naivety and ignorance on the inside.

There is so much evidence that supports that the emotional needs of a child, being heard and seen, are super critical to their self-esteem and self-worth as an adult; an important aspect of the Maslow's Hierarchy of needs[3]. I didn't know it yet but reflecting back, I see this is where my distress, anxiety and trauma actually began, which was extremely hard for a highly sensitive and caring person like me. Even back then, all of my unexpressed stress and emotions were subconsciously accumulating, and I had developed coping and/or survival mechanisms to protect myself from feeling more pain – perfection, being on high alert to the emotions of others, and doing anything and everything I could to please others so I felt approved of, liked and/or loved. They were automatically and subconsciously happening.

Like all young girls, I had a dream. A dream to meet my charming prince. A dream to live a peaceful, quiet, and beautiful life with the one I deeply, truly love. One day, it was shattered and that contributed to suicidal thoughts and an attempt to end my life that was miraculously stopped from happening. I was still unhealed, had no answers, no apology, denials and no closure, when a new adventure and a new door opened, and with a heavy heart, I left for Australia.

The onset of darkness and depression

Although I eventually humbly and graciously graduated with a Doctoral degree in Nutritional Food Sciences and became a subject-matter expert in the related field, I had to process my previously untouched emotional pains and traumas, which became even more prominent when I was alone in Australia with no support. Robin Sharma said:

'In the end. All YOU have is YOU. To Appreciate YOU when times are hard. To encourage YOU when YOU feel like surrendering.'

My healing journey during this chapter of my life was tremendously painful with episodes of anxiety and depression. I was constantly naively using my delicate, warm, sensitive and caring heart too much, trying to be in control to keep out of distress. I was giving too much of myself to people who did not appreciate me for who I am. I was never expressing my own needs, and was over giving to people who did not give back to me, and who wanted me to *'fit in'*, and *'be within their norms.'* Reflecting on how I was done wrong, stress upon stress built up. Crumbled, crippled, stumbled, destroyed to the core, torn apart into pieces, there was no place to go except into a deep depression. Hostility, wrath, and extreme all-over body pains (neck, shoulders, spinal, back, pelvic and menstrual pains) followed.

If this has happened or is happening to you too, it is paramount to take your pain, mental and emotional health seriously. Find and work closely with a health professional who takes this earnestly too.

To heal my own depression, and the aforementioned, associated excruciating body pains, I needed to authentically look into and tend to the root causes that led to them, so they didn't resurface again. The trauma and pent-up emotions needed to be completely freed and the behavioural patterns learned during childhood to gain acceptance and validation needed to be reframed. I needed to alter my relationships with my physical, mental and emotional bodies, respectively – to find, accept and love myself. To achieve that, I needed healing strategies. Amazingly, I found through many non-medical and non-pharmaceutical tools, depression, emotional wounds and chronic pains can be healed. These tools, not limited to, include eating consciously well, different kinds of conscious body movements, Yoga lifestyle, self-love and forgiveness practices, spirituality, body points pressing and boundary settings. Here are some of my favourite evidence-based practices.

Conscious body movement, singing, dancing, and un-learning NOT to cry, allowed me to take back my power

Singing and dancing to old love songs (Celine Dion, Mariah Carey, Whitney Houston, Toni Braxton, A.R. Rahman) were my life saviours that allowed me to unlock stagnated emotions and cry years of un-cried tears. Scientifically, crying is a powerful healing technique that unblocks suppressed emotions and helps remove toxins from our bodily systems[4]. Consciously moving my entire body, I moved and swayed gently, rhythmically and fluidly, feeling each and every move deeply, which allowed more tears to flow. If you want to try this yourself, drink a couple of glasses of warm water after you have finished and empty your bladder. Feel the lightness. FEEL IT. It's healing! You may also choose to have a soothing warm bath or shower. Even better, if the ocean is at your feet, and you're a swimmer, swim. Water is healing[5]. This creates a dilution process of emotions and toxins.

'Water is the driving force of all nature.'

Leonardo Da Vinci

All these started to turn things around. Then, when I realised that I needed to take charge and get myself out of all the mess, I calmed myself enough to listen and tune in. I also acknowledged that the psychosomatic pain symptoms taught me a great deal about what I needed to do less of (or more of) in my life to be content, peaceful, and healthy.

Huge relief and complete solace: Tapping to let go of pain and old stored up emotions

A strong believer in food as medicine and that our bodies know how to heal themselves, when painkillers and antidepressants were suggested to me, I screamed out a massive loud *'NO!!! You're NOT controlling me!'* Subconsciously and intuitively, I began gently tapping on my shoulders, neck, spine, all over my body, using the tips of my fingers, and my knuckles. It was a simple movement – a tapping – that softly activated the pressure points and the nerves all over my body to let go of any blockages. Intuitive movement at the end of this – shaking my body and dancing madly around – liberated so much more of the trapped emotions. Huge relief, complete solace, feeling the pains dissipating. EMOTION – E for Energy. So, getting the old, bound and blocked ENERGY into MOTION is something that I now regularly teach people.

Self-love and forgiveness of the past

Globally, there is a misconception that health is about nutrition – having balanced meals and the rainbow on our plates, exercise and good quality sleep. While all these factors are critical to good health and productivity, as a multidisciplinary Nutrition and Food Science Doctor, I can confidently share with you that it is a vicious cycle. Health is also what we feed into our mind, heart and skin – our thoughts, emotions and wounds. Hence, self-love and forgiveness essentially come into play. My health and episodes of pains would not have improved and I would not have re-written my story if it were not for three big things:

- Forgiving the past

- Being more grateful and happy about the present moment

- Giving myself the love I was desperately searching for from others while changing the ways I felt about and treated myself.

The daily practice of gratitude, Ho'Oponopono Prayer, and Yoga principles (asanas, pranayama and meditation) helped me do just that.

The Ho'Oponopono prayer is an ancient Hawaiian practice of forgiveness. It means to make things right. You can use this mantra as a reconciliation process for those you felt treated you badly in the past and/or as a tool for self-forgiveness and self-love.

The four simple, but extremely powerful lines of Ho'Oponopono are:

I am sorry.
Please forgive me.
I thank you.
I love you.

My overindulgence of food, loss of appetite and emotional eating combined with the emotional pain was severely impacting my menstrual health. I practised The Ho'Oponopono prayer to heal, and it did just that. Ask me how!

I now embrace this feminine and divine aspect of my core being. This prayer also helped me feel grounded, calm and self-accepting, as it is a complete form of self-love.

> **EXERCISE:** Repeat the above mantra anytime you are aware of a negative thought and/or emotion, but be warned, the Ho'Oponopono prayer works intensely and profoundly at the level of the subconscious mind. It brings out a lot of tears naturally … *so, prepare a box of tissues.*
>
> You can also follow the QR link to a sample of my gratitude journal prompts and a cheat sheet to find inner peace and happiness in the midst of life's chaos.

Yoga principles, the most fundamental tool in my healing and health practice

YOGA means UNION. Yoga is a tree and science of life that consists of eight important branches (limbs) to help bring equanimity in one's life. It is a powerful transformational tool that works a lot with the whirlpool of the activities of the mind (*vritti*). As stated in Chapter 1, Verse 2 of the Yoga Sutras, created by the Great Sage Maharishi Patanjali, YOGA is defined as *'the control and mastery of the fluctuations of the activities of the mind.'*

'Yogah Chitta Vritti Nirodhah' ||1.2||

Maharishi Patanjali

Yoga, a lifelong tool I encourage every parent to equip their child with from a very young age, something I wished I had learned earlier on. Yet, better late than never. Now, I endeavour to offer Yoga solutions to my clients in addition to conscious healthy eating, body movement and forgiveness. I do this because Yoga, in its TOTALITY, has considerably helped and protected me in various dimensions, and on all levels of my health; emotionally, physically, mentally, spiritually, energetically and socially. They include the following, but not limited to:

- Dissolving my anger through the Simhasana (The Lion Pose), showcasing the lioness's powerful qualities[6].

- Healing migraines, anxiety and depression[6,7].

- Teaching me to go deeply inward as all the resources to find true happiness are inside of me and NOT outward. Now, I'm content to be with myself. No attachments. Alone, happy and not lonely.

- Keeping my calm, maintaining silence *(Mauna)*, being kinder to, feeling, accepting and appreciating my body more and what it can do.

- Being very conscious about my postures, movement, breathing, words, actions, ways of eating, mind, thoughts and emotions.

- Focusing on the present moment through the power of breath.

- Eliminating toxins and wastes from the body that was due to the accumulated stress and over-indulgence. Now, no more overindulgence and emotional eating. I eat happily and consciously.

- Enhancing and deepening my connection with Mother Nature.

- Managing enormously my mood swings and menstruation health. No more menstrual pains.

- Speaking up, raising my voice confidently and assertively, and SAY NO through boundary settings, mantra chanting and chakra healing.

- PAUSING and BREATHING, before I say YES.

- Alleviating my fear, self-doubt and lack of self-confidence while building resilience.

There are so many more positive benefits that Yoga practices have brought to my life. If you do anything for yourself, your mental health, depression, emotions and bodily pains, *Do Yoga!* YOGA is the ultimate answer to everything.

Setting boundaries to protect my beautiful light

Boundary setting was a massive part of my learning curve and that is because setting healthy boundaries allows me to:

- Control and protect myself from emotional pains and resentment.

- Speak up for myself, speak my truth and NOT just say YES to everyone and everything.

- Stand up for myself and set limits to what is right for me.

- Get out of painful situations quickly as soon as I see red lights, and not to linger on because of my values of being sincere and loyal.

- NOT to try to fix people and things anymore at the expense of my own health.

Boundary setting is a form of loving, respecting, caring and speaking up for oneself. It is about stopping *'being nice'* whilst continuing to be a good person. There is a huge difference between *'nice'* and being *'good'*. Being *'nice'* and having too much sincerity and serenity got me used, stressed out, disrespected, and only temporary validation and approval. Being *'good'* means being authentic, honouring your truths, taking care of your needs without compromising your core values. Ladies! In case you need to hear this today; this is not selfishness! This is a part of self-care. It is such a valuable and critical concept that I wish I had learned during my childhood, and yet greatly helps a person to:

- Set clear guidelines, rules and limits on what one feels is right and not right.

- Move away from any life circumstances that are not serving oneself.

- Feel protected, respected, comfortable, and safe.

- Develop self-compassion and compassion for others.

- Honour one's needs and wants without feeling guilty and shameful.

- Understand how one would like to be treated.

Prior to being able to set my limits, I had to give myself permission to tap into this new habit. I utilised my research skills to discover and develop new evidence-based tools, and consistently did my homework (Figure 1).

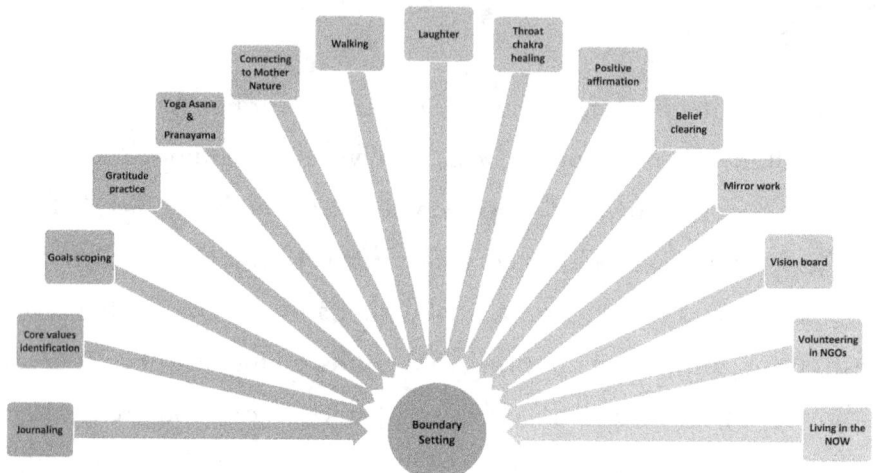

Figure 1: Internal homework that led to the pathway of setting boundaries smoothly.

A couple of other boundary setting tools that I used when saying NO confidently, without second-guessing, justifying, over-explaining myself, and any regrets, include:

- Depending on the situation(s), using 'I' statements, without any form of accusation or blaming, say *'I'm sorry to hear. Thank you for sharing with me. I'd like to help you out but let me check my schedule, and I'll get back to you.'*

- In any given situation that is NOT SOOTHING and NOURISHING TO YOUR SOUL, you have a choice to walk away, knowing that it is OKAY to walk away.

- Listen to your gut feeling - that butterfly sensation in the stomach/chest/heart, it says a lot. Listen to it.

- Don't make assumptions (3*rd* *of The Four Agreements by Don Miguel Ruiz*) – remember questioning was not a thing during my childhood. Now, I ask questions and look for clarification, which is outside of my comfort zone, but Brené Brown says: *'Choose discomfort over resentment.'*

- Write down 'SAY NO' on a piece of paper, and stick in my wallet, phone casing, and on the walls to remind myself, rewire my brain and help rewrite my story. Brené Brown also mentions, *'Like many worthwhile endeavours, boundary setting is a practice. So, REHEARSE!!!'*

What are you willing to try this week? Could you try some body movements, Yoga practices, setting boundaries or forgiveness?

Stars do not shine brightly without darkness

I am a living example that stars do not shine without darkness. I have experienced it all, and now I have an amazing level of understanding of how it feels, and how painful it is. So, now I can share tools that work effectively with you so you, too, heal and experience long-lasting positive effects. As a student of life, humble and conscientious single, never married lady, who understands life hardships in all its dimensions, I now live in alignment with my life purpose of merging my acquired multidisciplinary knowledge and wisdom to promote and advocate for 8 important pillars of health, raising awareness, and serving people to preclude and manage the onset of preventable diseases and chronic pains. Identifying root causes of physical, mental and emotional health problems and chronic pains, I help women with my unique person-centred holistic approach, within a safe, confidential and non-judgemental space. Beautiful people – never give up, persevere and remember this powerful quote from Charlie Chaplin, for your deeper personal contemplation.

'Nothing is permanent in this world, not even our troubles.'
Charlie Chaplin

References

1. Rikard, S.M., Strahan, A.E., Schmit, K.M., & Guy, G.P. (2023). Chronic pain among adults - United States, 2019 - 2021. *Morbidity and Mortality Weekly Report*. 72(15): 379-385. doi: 10.15585/mmwr.mm7215a1.

2. Clouser, G. (2022). *Oh, the Aches and Pains*. Yale School of Medicine. Retrieved on 12 Oct 2024. https://medicine.yale.edu/news-article/oh-the-aches-and-pains/.

3. Williams, D.E., & Page, M.M. (1989). A multi-dimensional measure of Maslow's hierarchy of needs. *Journal of Research in Personality*. 23(2), 192-213. https://doi.org/10.1016/0092-6566(89)90023-8.

4. Gutjahr, F., & Benecke, C. (2024). Crying in psychotherapy: an exploratory mixed-methods study on forms of emotional crying and associated therapeutic interventions. *Research in Psychotherapy*. 27(1): 725. doi: 10.4081/ripppo.2024.725.

5. Becker, B., Hildenbrand, K., Whitcomb, R.K., Sanders, J.P. (2009). Biophysiologic effects of warm water immersion. *International Journal of Aquatic Research and Education.* 3(1). Article 4. https://doi.org/10.25035/ijare.03.01.04.

6. Javed, D., & Mishra, S. (2022). Yoga practices in Social Anxiety Disorder (SAnD): A case report WSR to paruresis. *Journal of Ayurved and Integrative Medicine.* 13(3). https://doi.org/10.1016/j.jaim.2022.100622.

7. Nanthakumar, C. (2020). Yoga for anxiety and depression - a literature review. *The Journal of Mental Health Training, Education and Practice.* 15(3), 157-169. https://doi.org/10.1108/JMTEP-09-2019-0050.

Chapter Fifteen

Life Is a Puzzle

6 Million reasons to find your worth, health and wellness.

> With Lida Johnson, certified nutritionist, health and wellness coach, and founder of Head-to-Toe Coaching and the #6MillionReasons movement.

Do you find it hard to feel good about yourself? Do you often compare yourself to others, feeling inadequate or less than?

There are 6 million reasons to let your inner light shine, yet we often let self-imposed doubts overshadow them. We are all born worthy – a majestic masterpiece – but life's challenges can make us forget our true value, shaping how we see ourselves and how we live.

Addressing your health and wellness isn't just about willpower, exercise, or diet – it's a complex puzzle shaped by every aspect of your life. Childhood traumas, whether big or seemingly minor, leave lasting imprints that influence your thoughts, behaviours, and even physical health. These experiences can't simply be ignored; they linger and quietly affect how you view yourself and the world. Healing begins by acknowledging these wounds as part of your journey. Only then can you truly move forward.

Growing up in an abusive, alcoholic family, I myself struggled with negative self-worth, low self-esteem, self-loathing, compulsive overeating, and sugar addiction. It wasn't until I embraced a holistic wellness journey that I began to reclaim my life. Now, I help others navigate their own health and wellness challenges by piecing together their unique puzzles.

Self-care is the most important thing you can do for your health and well-being. It shows yourself – and the world – that you matter. When you exercise, limit screen time, rest, and treat your body and mind with kindness, you affirm that you are worthy of care, happiness, and health. You deserve to thrive.

Putting together the pieces of your life – discovering your true self, embracing your worth, and achieving lasting health and wellness – is like solving a giant puzzle. With proven systems and techniques, you can create positive daily habits that go beyond sheer willpower. Join me, as I guide you through this transformative journey.

Nothing more than a piece of trash

My early childhood was marked by verbal and physical abuse, emotional struggles, and addiction, that left me with scars for life, but the real 'aha' I-am-a-piece-of-trash, kind of moment came at this time …

I had just returned to the United States after spending my senior year of high school as an exchange student in Denmark. I went to visit my stepmother and sister to collect my belongings since I was going to live with my dad. My parents had divorced, while I was living abroad that year. This was my first time visiting my stepmother since the divorce, and I was told she had kept my childhood things.

When I asked for them, my sister came out with a copy paper box – roughly 17.5 inches long, 11.5 inches deep, and 18 inches high.

Inside that small space were the remnants of 17 years of life as one of three children, a father, and a stepmother. There are no crayon drawings from my early years, the kind that might have once decorated the refrigerator before being carefully tucked away. No cherished souvenirs from family vacations. No tiny baby teeth were saved by sentimental parents. No beloved stuffed animals or toys that brought comfort during hard times. School report cards and projects are absent from the box. No pictures capturing family moments.

When I asked about the rest of my things, my stepmother replied, *'I don't know. Maybe thrown out with the trash.'*

Those words echoed in my mind, over and over – *'thrown out with the trash.'*

The silence that followed felt like an eternity as if all the air had been sucked out of the room. In the past, my words had been my shield, my defence against a world that often felt overwhelming. But in that moment, when it mattered most, I had no words. I couldn't even move.

In those few seconds, I was completely shattered. I felt utterly worthless and invisible, like nothing more than a piece of trash – easily discarded by the very people who should have loved and protected me the most.

Overwhelmed by a whirlwind of thoughts and emotions – even rage – I could barely manage to say, *'I've got to go.'* I turned and walked away, clutching that small, lightweight box, silently repeating to myself, *'I hate my life. I hate myself. I don't trust anyone.'*

But then came a resolve: *'I'm never going to feel this way again.'*

Have you ever held onto a core belief or story that shaped a negative view of yourself and your future, making happiness seem impossible? I thought I was destined to be miserable.

Hope, the possibility of change

After nearly a decade of merely existing, a series of events led me to embark on a transformative thru-hike of the Appalachian Trail (AT), a 2,200-mile journey across 14 states of the USA from Georgia to Maine.

Over six months, much of it spent alone, I pushed my physical and mental limits, gradually reconnecting with myself. Along the way, I encountered genuine kindness from strangers who treated me like family, offering support and encouragement.

As I walked, the persistent negativity from within and around me began to fade. In the newfound silence, I discovered an inner strength and a glimmer of hope. I began to believe that I was deserving of love, health, and well-being and that I didn't need to carry the weight of self-doubt any longer.

Like a puzzle: Your health & well-being

I've always had a natural gift for assembling puzzles. I typically start with the edges to create the outer framework that guides the rest of the process. In many ways, health and wellness follow a similar path. You begin with the foundational elements and then from there, you carefully place each piece, where each one represents a critical aspect of your well-being such as physical health, mental clarity, emotional resilience, or social connections. Every piece is essential and together they form the bigger picture.

Just as assembling a puzzle requires patience and persistence, so does the journey of self-care and personal growth. Whether you're working to overcome self-doubt, build confidence, or enhance your mental, physical, and social well-being, each step forward is like placing another piece in the puzzle. Slowly but steadily, you create a complete, vibrant picture of health – one that is uniquely yours, built piece by piece with care, intention, and dedication.

Your values: Your guiding star

The outer border or the foundational elements are your values – the core of who you are, representing your ideals and unique self. They are the beliefs and desired outcomes that transcend specific circumstances. Values shape your life's vision and guide your actions and decisions and, when consistently practised, define the character you want to embody. Without them, you're adrift and reactive.

Before I began my well-being journey, I had no idea what my values were. They were dictated by others. Now, my values guide my dreams, set my boundaries, and define my essence. Let's take some time to discover what your values are.

> **EXERCISE: Hone in on your values**
>
> 1. Ground yourself in a quiet place. Relax. Empty your mind.
>
> 2. Let go of all preconceived notions, especially past stories and with a

curious mind think about the future.

3. Brainstorm a list of personal values – go crazy. Refer to my list of values if you like.

4. Group the values under related themes.

5. Highlight central themes, there may be several, into one word.

Values

Integrity
Honesty
Compassion
Courage
Respect
Responsibility
Kindness
Empathy
Loyalty
Humility
Gratitude
Generosity
Fairness
Patience
Perseverance
Forgiveness
Justice
Trustworthiness
Self-discipline
Ambition
Wisdom
Curiosity
Open-mindedness
Optimism
Innovation
Creativity
Diligence
Accountability

Reliability
Commitment
Humility
Faith
Hope
Love
Altruism
Compassion
Selflessness
Tolerance
Inclusivity
Unity
Peace
Service
Honor
Simplicity
Balance
Mindfulness
Authenticity
Flexibility
Determination
Dedication
Excellence
Independence
Freedom
Stability
Moderation

Resilience
Adaptability
Health
Well-being
Growth
Learning
Self-improvement
Cooperation
Collaboration
Family
Friendship
Community
Tradition
Legacy
Sustainability
Stewardship
Environmentalism
Respect for Nature
Adventure
Exploration
Passion
Zeal
Enthusiasm
Justice
Advocacy
Truth
Honesty

Honesty
Transparency
Clarity
Prudence
Modesty
Sincerity
Contentment
Harmony
Forgiveness
Charity
Purpose
Vision
Focus
Determination
Ambition
Spirit
Empowerment
Inclusiveness
Mutual Respect
Spirituality
Adaptability
Altruism
Compassion
Contentment
Decisiveness
Inclusivity
Insightfulness

 Lida@headtotoecoaching.com
www.headtotoecoaching.com

With your values in place, you can start focusing on the different sections or pillars of the puzzle that make up your overall health and well-being. Some areas may come into focus more quickly than others, but don't worry – it's normal for your priorities to shift as life evolves. Remember, your health and wellness is a journey, not a destination.

As you explore the various aspects of your health and well-being, be gentle with yourself. Each area is complex, with many nuances – like puzzle pieces that take time and patience to fit together.

Mental wellness is crucial

I used to wake up tired and cranky and with a negative mindset before the day even began. What about you? Is your first thought in the morning positive, neutral, or negative?

Your mindset shapes your day and affects your overall outlook on life. It influences how you see yourself, handle challenges, and interact with others. Our brains naturally focus on negative experiences due to an evolutionary trait called negativity bias, which once helped ensure our survival. But today, this bias can keep us stuck in negative thought patterns.

I've faced severe mental health challenges – self-doubt, worthlessness, and a desire to hide from the world. Mental wellness was the hardest part of my personal puzzle to solve and stay consistent with. This is not uncommon and often where people get stuck on their health and wellness journey.

Are you stuck in a cycle of negative thoughts or actions?

> **Tips for practicing positivity**
>
> 1. Gratitude journal – write 3 to 5 things you are thankful for in the morning and evening.
>
> 2. Spend time outside, every day if possible.
>
> 3. Engage in joyful activities.
>
> 4. Manage Negative Emotions. Address stress, anxiety, and other negative emotions. Remember, acknowledging these feelings doesn't mean you have to dwell on them.

Physical well-being

Our thoughts about movement are influenced by many factors, including self-doubt, negativity, and even our diet. On the other hand, a positive mindset, sufficient sleep, and thoughtful planning are key to staying motivated. For me, exercise has always been a sanctuary – a cornerstone of my health that usually comes naturally, yet, at times, it still presents challenges.

Both movement and physical activity are crucial for overall health and wellness. Physical activity serves as a powerful form of medicine, protecting your heart, boosting your metabolism, and helping to prevent disease. Movement, however, is the lifeblood of your well-being, fuelling both your body and mind. Simple actions like walking the dog and taking in your surroundings aren't technically exercise, but they open the door to a healthier, longer life. This is why you need both – physical activity to strengthen your body and movement to nurture your vitality.

Where do you stand? Do you embrace movement? Do you find yourself saying, *'I hate to exercise?'* Maybe you know you need to move more but aren't sure how to start.

> **Tips for physical activity**
>
> 1. Keep it simple.
>
> 2. Move in ways you love.
>
> 3. Play and have fun.
>
> 4. Schedule activities on your calendar—and include others for accountability.
>
> 5. Get outside daily to enhance clarity, focus, and reduce stress and anxiety.

Nutrition and diet

I've fallen into diet culture many times, trying different diets that often compromised my health, strained my relationships, and led to self-sabotaging behaviours. As a kid, I used food to bury my emotions. I was addicted to sugar, and vegetables were a rarity in our meals, so changing my eating habits has been a significant and ongoing challenge.

Relying solely on willpower to control food intake is unsustainable because we only have a limited amount of willpower to cover all the decisions we make each day. This often leads to a frustrating cycle of losing and regaining weight, never feeling confident that any progress will last.

Nutrition and diet are also tangled in a cultural narrative of *'why can't you just...'*. When I shifted my focus to everything else in my life – relationships, well-being, career, and spirituality to start – the importance of the actual food I was eating diminished. Food became fuel, no longer a crutch for boredom, stress, anxiety, or overwhelm.

It's important to remember that what works for one person may not work for you. What's healthy for someone else could be harmful to you. Your reasons for eating, along with when, where, and how you eat, all play a crucial role in your well-being. When the other pillars of health and wellness are in balance, it becomes easier to eat with the primary focus on fuelling your body.

As humans, we're not perfect, and neither is your approach to eating. Learning to eat in a way that nourishes your body takes practice and self-compassion. Enjoy that treat without guilt, and avoid falling into the trap of thinking, *'I blew it, so I'll start again on Monday.'* Instead, get back on track as soon as possible, and be kind to yourself along the way.

What should I eat?

1. Whole foods.

2. Avoid processed and added sugar.

3. Drink plenty of water.

4. Eat intuitively.

Dream It. Believe It. Do It.

There are many aspects of health and wellness that go beyond what I've mentioned in this brief story – sleep, environment, finances, career, spirituality, clutter, and more. Education, practice, and having a feedback loop play a key role in your health journey, acting as the thread that ties all the pieces together.

I've come to understand that trauma, whether major or seemingly minor, leaves a lasting imprint on our lives. It lingers in the background, shaping our thoughts, behaviours, and even our physical health. These experiences can't just be swept under the rug or forgotten, despite what others might suggest. They persist, quietly influencing how you view the world and yourself. Ignoring them only strengthens their hold, gradually chipping away at your sense of self-worth and overall well-being. Healing begins with acknowledging and addressing these wounds – only then can you truly move forward.

Your unique puzzle is a complex mosaic shaped by your experiences and emotions. It's crucial to understand who you are, what you stand for, and the beliefs you hold. This intricate combination of elements makes you whole, reminding you that every piece, whether light or dark, has its place in the puzzle of life.

As you work on your life puzzle, some pieces will come into focus quickly, while others remain blurry. And like a puzzle, our health and wellness is interconnected, with a constant push and pull between the various pillars. Consistent practice is what ultimately determines your overall wellness.

When I hear someone say, *'I can't change {fill in the blank},'* I know that's not true – I'm living proof that you can. As a coach, I lead with love. You may not believe in yourself yet, but I believe in you.

Tips for piecing this all together

1. Find your north star

2. Practise mental well-being strategies

3. Be active daily

4. Fuel your body, not your emotions

If you are ready to start your health and wellness journey and want some amazing free tools to kick start your journey, scan the QR to sign up for the Triple-E Newsletter, and I will automatically send you a Goal-Setting Worksheet, Meal Prep Guide, Grocery Store List and a Food, Feelings, Function Diary.

MAKING THINGS RIGHT

Processes for giving yourself the care and compassion, you naturally and automatically give to others.

Chapter Sixteen

Ho'oponopono – Making Things Right

The power of self-forgiveness in creating a more fulfilled and authentic life.

With creator of *Lead with Love* Adie McDermott.

Forgiveness, especially self-forgiveness, is super hard. However, when we do it, it frees us from so much old resentment, anger, sadness, bitterness and shame. Unforgiveness on the other hand can create pain and disease in the body, affect our emotional wellbeing, keep us stuck and hold us back from living a life we desire and deserve.

According to Brainz Magazine author Thersea Agostinelli:

> '*There can be many feelings associated with creating your own future, such as fear, regret, guilt, and more. This makes forgiveness very difficult. Whether unforgiveness is passed on from generation to generation or from previous bad experiences, it is imperative to be aware of your mindset. You have the power to stop the constant reminders of the past and look toward*

the future and learn to forgive others and yourself. Changing your mindset can help you to create new ways of thinking that support the life you dream about. Only when we free ourselves of past mistakes and make peace with where we are right now, will we truly embrace our future and live the most abundant and amazing life we could ever dream about.'

Ho'oponopono (pronounced <u>Ho-oh-po-no-po-no</u>) is an ancient Hawaiian practice of forgiveness and one of my favourite ways to give myself some compassion and love. Ho'oponopono means to make things right. You can use this mantra as a reconciliation and forgiveness process for those you felt treated you badly in the past, or as a tool for self-forgiveness, self-love.

The four simple, but super powerful lines of Ho'oponopono are:

I am sorry
Please forgive me
Thankyou
I love you

I also love to add in the lines:

I forgive you
and I set you free.

In life we don't just create art, performances, poetry and music, we create everything in our lives with our own thoughts. Our reactions to things create our emotions, our beliefs and our reality, how we feel about ourselves, others and our lives. (Some people say) Thoughts are so powerful that our thoughts determine what our life will be like, and/or how we will feel next.

Ho'oponopono crowds out self-critical thoughts, and if you do it enough, creates new, kinder beliefs about ourselves.

Our brain is very smart, powerful and a bit backwards (behind the times) at the same time. It gets addicted to feeling a certain way if that way is harmful to our mental health and self-esteem, does not like change even if it's good for us and puts up a fight when you try to be better.

It does not distinguish between right and wrong, fact or fiction. It believes you every time you tell yourself you are not good enough, that your life is no good or that something bad may happen.

Experts say we have up to 60,000 thoughts a day, 90% of them are repeated over and over again and 70% of them are negative.

All day we mostly hold onto, get stuck on and replay thoughts from the past and we worry about our future.

But with awareness of what is going on we can make changes. Just because we think something doesn't mean it is the truth. Thoughts are thoughts only, not the truth. We can change how we feel about ourselves and our lives by crowding them out with other more positive ones. This will take time but it will eventually settle in and feel natural.

If you want to use this as a self-forgiveness meditation, as you say the mantras add your name. If you have someone else you want to forgive, say their name. Forgiveness of others releases old emotions you are carting around with you like resentment and anger, which is also an act of self-love. After you say the words, become aware of the thoughts that arise and add these thoughts in.

For example:

I am sorry (insert your name) – I have been treating you so badly.
Please forgive me – for that
Thankyou – for being exactly as you are
I love you – wholeheartedly, exactly as you are
I forgive you – for not being perfect. For not getting everything right
I set you free – to be yourself, to be happy, to be loved, to be …?

If you are not used to doing this or saying kind things to yourself this will feel VERY weird and you will also most certainly feel like a fraud. Remember your brain likes feeling how it does and does not like change, even positive change. You will probably hear resistance to what you are saying, by hearing things like, *'yeah right, as if'*, and *'you have got to be kidding'* etc.

Afterwards your mind also can become super mean in a more exaggerated way as it is trying madly to reverse the good you have done. Thinking *'my mind is selling me a bag of lies right now'* is helpful, and also remembering that this is all normal and changes over time until it becomes more natural. It is also important to remember everything you do here is for your benefit, so please try not to beat yourself up for not getting everything right, getting distracted, your thoughts going off in another direction etc., this happens to everyone. When you notice this simply just come back to the mantra.

Ho'oponopono Forgiveness Meditation:

Listen and follow along to a Ho'oponopono forgiveness meditation that I created in collaboration with my sound healing trained sister Louise McDermott here.

References

- https://www.brainzmagazine.com/post/the-power-of-self-forgiveness-path-to-healing

Chapter Seventeen

Re-discovering Joy in Midlife

How your inner child holds the keys to your happiness and quality of life as an adult and how to get to know her.

With creator of *Lead with Love* Adie McDermott.

'I started calling that girl back. The girl who loved living, the girl who danced instead of walking.
The girl who had sunflowers for eyes and fireworks in her soul.
I started playing music again, hoping she would come out.
I started looking for beautiful moments to experience, so she would feel safe enough to show herself, because I knew she was in there.
And she needed my kindness and my effort to come to the surface again.'

S.C. Lourie: 'Butterflies and Pebbles'

Midlife can be a positive transformational time in a woman's life, but it often comes with its share of challenges. According to experts and in this case, Sandra Roach Coaching *The exhaustion, depression and feelings of failure that some midlife women experience can be overwhelming, but it's important to remember that this phase can also be an opportunity for growth, self-discovery and a chance for a fresh outlook on life'.*

In my experience our inner child holds the keys to our happiness and quality of our life as an adult.

An inner child lives within all of us, it's the part of us that is playful, intuitive and creative. Usually hidden under our grown-up personas, our ego and our adult perfectionism, our inner child not only holds the keys to our joy in life as an adult, she holds the keys to what's been holding us back all our life.

I personally communicate with, and give voice to mine every time I create art, walk on the beach or in nature, walk in the rain, ride my bike through puddles and hang out with kids. There are many other ways you can do that for yourself too.

To avoid pain from the past, you have probably tried hard most of your life to ignore your inner child, but… you know what? She never goes away. Our inner child lives in our unconscious mind and influences how we make choices, respond to challenges, and live our lives every day.

When you start to listen to your inner child you gift yourself JOY, self-compassion and self-acceptance. You also heal by giving yourself today the things you wish others had given you in childhood.

Everybody experiences some sort of trauma and shame from childhood. *Everybody!* But through journaling, creativity and visualisations you can go back and give the child the love you needed and didn't receive and can heal the past so your present and your future looks brighter.

Among other things giving voice to your inner your child allows you to:

- Experience pure joy and freedom again

- Give yourself what you didn't get from others as a child

- Open up your imagination

- Unlock your inner joy, inner creativity, curiosity, wonder, optimism and ... your limitless ability to love

- Bring more magic into your life

- Feel self-compassion, rediscover yourself, value and have confidence in yourself

- Access and heal repressed memories and stories that are holding you back

- Rediscover who you are, what you love and what brings you joy

- Be able to feel again after many years of being numb

- Gain more self-knowledge and personal power and increase your ability to set boundaries

- Learn how to value and take care of yourself

- Improve intimacy in relationships

- Stop recreating or reacting to the past.

Being playful in any way gives our inner child love. You can give her even more by finding out what she needs and going back in time and loving her up. Giving her hugs, love and the things that she did not get as a child. Using visualisations to do this is what scientists call neuro or brain reprogramming and it has been proven by scientific studies to change your subconscious beliefs and how you feel about yourself.

How can you get to know your inner child, nurture her and give her love?:

- Take small moments of listening to and respecting your inner child in your life by doing something that by our adult mind seems childish. When you respect her and allow her to come out and play without judgement you are showing her that you see her, hear her, love her and care. These things could be scribbling all over your page, flicking paint and making a mess in an art practice, dancing wildly, singing at the top of your lungs, walking barefoot on the beach, skipping or running in and out of waves, riding your bike through puddles etc.

- Stillness: Practice breathwork, mindfulness and meditation, anything that allows you to slow down so you can listen to your own inner voice.

- Allow yourself to play, nurture your creativity, get things wrong and make a mess.

- Learn to 'reparent' yourself, e.g. listen to your inner child to learn how to nurture and care for yourself, then do it.

- Use a writing journal to communicate with her. Use the journal as a safe space to express yourself honestly. Ask your inner child how she's feeling today. Honour her feelings and perception of experiences without filtering or correcting them.

- Ask her: 'What do you need that I'm not making space for?' 'Where am I currently leaving you out?'

- Ask her things like what did she always want to be growing up?

- What are her favourite memories? What she wished she'd had, or had more of, as a child. Does she wish she had more attention, more love, more time to play with her parents, more freedom to express herself, play and enjoy being a child, respect, guidance, acceptance, encouragement, acknowledgment, or something else?

Be aware that this type of work can bring up strong emotions, like hidden sadness, anger, regret, resentment, longing and bitterness, so if you feel out of your depth please consult a qualified therapist, not do this all alone.

The process of visualisation is a great way to connect to your inner child. After you identify through journaling what you wish you'd had, or had more of, as a child, go back and give yourself what you need using visualisation.

Visualisations help us to gradually re-write and recreate our beliefs and live better in the present. The best time to do visualisations is when your brain is in a super absorbent relaxed mode. Just before bed, first thing when you wake up in the morning and during meditation.

When you feel totally relaxed ...

Visualise yourself as a young child. Hug and hold that child. Tell her you love her, that she is beautiful and that you accept her as she is. Assure her nothing that happened to you was your fault. Tell her what she needs to hear.

For example:

'I love you'
'I am here for you, and I am listening, tell me what you need to feel safe or happy'
'You are sooo beautiful'
'Don't ever stop shining your light'
'I am sorry'
'You are enough exactly how you are'
'You are safe, You are loved'
'You are seen, you are heard and you are loved for who you are'

You can also visualise her receiving what she did not receive from your parents or guardians. Perhaps them telling her that she is beautiful, not flawed, that they love her and that whatever is going on around her is not her fault.

I also adore this *Hidden Joys* exercise from my creative healing membership *Whole* – that helps find your hidden joys.

> *'The most potent muse of all is our own inner* child.'
> Stephen Nachmanovitch

The childhood hopes and dreams we had when we were younger may right now seem imaginary, made-up, pointless or insignificant to you, but they are actually very important missing parts of us that need to be honoured for us to lead our most joyful, creative and fulfilled lives.

Inspired by Julia Cameron's *The Artists Way*, the following questions are designed to find what joys, gifts or imaginary lives were left behind or pushed to the side in order to conform to society or grow up.

In a selfish, or a time and money unlimited world, I would suggest you to go out and try all these new things to narrow them down to the ones you like the best. If that is not very practical to you, instead consider how you can bring parts of this into your life now. For example, if you discover you always wanted to be a drummer for example, take some weekly or monthly drumming lessons.

- What did you love to do when you were younger? *Draw imaginary characters, play make-believe games, run in and out of waves at the ocean etc.*

- What would you try if it weren't too selfish? *Take a solo pampering sojourn to Bali or Thailand, take a meditation course, write and illustrate a children's book, walk the Camino trail etc.*

- If you could relive your life 3 times over again, and there were no limits to what you could do in them, what would you do or be? E.g. become an artist, a monk, a circus performer, a scuba diving instructor, a ballet dancer, a famous tennis player etc.?

- What did you love to do as a child that is not appropriate to do now?

- What were you not allowed to be, or do as a child that you would love to do now?

- What would you love to try if it weren't too crazy? *Climb Mount*

Everest, fly to Mars, sell my house and go sailing around the world etc.

- If there were no limits to what you would or could do or be? How would you live? Let your imagination run wild here.

To begin, choose a few things to bring into your life and see if they do, or do not bring you joy. If they do, keep doing them, if they don't, try something else. As a woman, a mother, a wife, a sister, a daughter, a friend and a worker (sometimes) all in one time, you lead a busy life ... but you deserve this joyous play time!

References

- https://sandradcoaching.com/blog/rediscover-joy-transforming-midlife-perspective?format=amp

- https://www.mindbodygreen.com/search?q=Inner+child

- https://www.harleytherapy.co.uk/counselling/inner-child-work-can-benefit.htm

- https://juliacameronlive.com/

SHARING YOUR VOICE

Speak to heal, speak with love
and speak your truth.

Chapter Eighteen

The Fine Art of Being Seen

The role self-esteem, self-expression and self-compassion play in being seen, heard and loved for who you are.

> With creator of *Lead with Love* Adie McDermott: an internationally published expert in self-expression and self-compassion, and a multi-disciplinary creative who creates programs and spaces all over the world where women can express themselves so their *'true'* voices are heard and seen.

'I believe one of the bravest and most important journeys we are on in this lifetime is learning the truth, which is that we are more than enough, and knowing, and believing it in every part of our being'.

Jamie Kern Lima, Author of WORTHY

It's hard for me to put into words, the overwhelming joy and gratitude I feel at being able to stand in my power, express myself, allow love and joy into my life and allow myself be seen and heard all around the world, after a lifetime of co-dependency, serious self-loathing, giving myself away and not allowing myself to be loved, seen or heard.

The truth is, extreme loneliness, anger and fear were my best friends and worst enemies for almost 50 years. As an undiagnosed neuro-divergent person, who formed the belief at a very young age that it was never okay to express their emotions or needs, there were so many things to fear. Loud noises and angry voices, the darkness and anything unknown, smells, bright lights (especially if they were flashing), things moving fast and all at once, my own huge feelings, chronic unexplained pain in my body, things that I could not control, change, other people's negative feelings because I could (and can still) feel them as if they were my own, speaking in front of anyone, not understanding or being understood, social situations especially big groups and for many years any 1-1 interaction, and of course making friends and meeting new people in general.

My biggest fear however has always been *the fear of rejection*. A deep rejection sensitivity dysphoria, which manifested in me as very low self-esteem and worth, a desperate need to be perfect, get everything right all the time, silencing my needs to ensure I was accommodating and super pleasing so I was approved of, liked and loved; huge self-loathing and debilitating shame if I ever believed I was not; and completely shutting down my heart, as life was far less hurtful that way.

While I longed to feel loved and day-dreamed for my whole life of being world renowned, I had a deep fear of and resistance to actually being *seen* and being *loved*. These fears have seen me constantly (subconsciously) looking for reasons why someone is or will inevitably reject me; not wanting to be close to people; putting my needs to the back of everyone else's; feeling desperately alone for most of my life; chasing friendships with people who do not see me; being in unhealthy relationships with people (addicts) that could not love me; and not putting myself out there for new jobs, promotions or business opportunities.

I was genetically disposed to rejection sensitivity dysphoria, but I know I am not alone in experiencing the fear of rejection and of being truly seen. Rejection sensitivity is often also a learned response. MANY people are held back from leading a life they desire and deserve because they do not realise this, understand what this means, and that they can change.

If you are reading this, there's a good chance you feel these fears too.

So, why is it hard for most of us to be truly seen, neurodivergent or not? It all comes down to the beliefs you formed during childhood around expressing yourself, how safe you and your own nervous system feel expressing yourself, and how you feel about, value, speak to and treat yourself – your self-esteem, your self-worth and your self-compassion.

Low self-esteem kills confidence and stops us expressing ourselves

According to thriveworks.com, *'feelings of self-worth and self-esteem come from one's self-concept. Plainly put, self-concept is the way one thinks about themselves.'* This is brilliant news, as this means we are in control of this self-concept, and we can change this and create a new identity for ourselves. But first, let's have a look at my favourite ways why and how we feel about ourselves were formed:

Society in general has a lot to blame for why we ALL have trouble expressing and showing ourselves.

- Growing up, our parents teach us to be polite and pleasing, leading to low self-esteem and worth, feelings of not being good enough and worthy of being seen or heard.

- Schools teach us that being the same as everyone else is the way to fit in and not get in trouble – leading to low self-esteem.

- Secondary schools have tests and examinations, where there is only one answer to questions and problems. If we do not get them right, we are wrong, or a failure – leading to more low self-esteem.

- As humans we are wired to be loved and to belong. Somewhere along the way, we ourselves make the decision, influenced by others and the world around us, that it is not smart or safe to be ourselves, that we must change to fit in.

- As women, our voices are silenced from a very young age and we are socially conditioned to please others, be perfect and do the 'right thing'. These pleasing behaviours stop us from allowing ourselves to be seen and heard.

So much research also states that self-esteem begins during childhood and I strongly agree with this view from uthealtheasttexas.com that says it *'results from hearing or interpreting messages from significant people including parents, siblings, friends and teachers, who were often very critical. This type of feedback results in thoughts such as 'I'm not good enough,' 'I'm not loveable,' or feeling as if they are unable to live up to others or their own expectations.'*

If you experienced any kind of childhood trauma, abuse or simply a parent who was controlling, emotionally distant or absent for any reason – death, addiction, mental health, working a lot, relationship breakup – you will understand when I say that it felt like you were not loveable enough to be seen or heard; to feel constantly unsafe, and to feel like life was out of your control.

One of the biggest things most children experience even in very caring families is emotional invalidation. As a highly sensitive child who felt very strong emotions, I longed for my parents to acknowledge what I was feeling, listen and to show that they understood.

All these things that happen in childhood are a very strong recipe for low self-esteem and worth as an adult. You might now experience shame around showing or asserting yourself, self-criticism, perfectionism, undervaluing yourself, exhaustion, unhealthy relationships – and even an income level that you can't bump up, no matter how much you learn, or how hard you work?

Dr Jonice Webb states it in a way I feel deeply in my body:

> *Just like adults, children's feelings are the deepest, most personal, biological expression of who they are. In order to feel seen, understood, and heard, a child must feel that their feelings are seen, understood, and heard. If your parents didn't have the emotional awareness or emotional skills to see and accept what you were feeling, they may have, perhaps of no fault of their own, failed to validate you. As a result, you may have grown up to feel unseen, misunderstood, and unheard. You may feel less valid than everyone else'.*

Making the subconscious conscious: Become curious to where and how you are keeping yourself hidden and small so you can heal it

There are so many layers to allowing yourself to be seen, heard. The truth is, you cannot consciously will yourself to express yourself more. You need to do the work. I totally relate to this list of how a 'typical' person with low self-esteem is from betterhealth.vic.gov.au:

Typically, a person with low self-esteem:

- Is extremely critical of themselves.

- Downplays or ignores their positive qualities.

- Judges themselves to be inferior to their peers.

- Uses negative words to describe themselves such as stupid, fat, ugly or unlovable.

- Has discussions with themselves (this is called 'self-talk') that are always negative, critical and self-blaming.

- Blames themselves when things go wrong instead of taking into account other things over which they have no control such as the actions of other people or economic forces.

- Doesn't believe a person who compliments them.

But, a lot of ways and reasons why you are stuck and keeping yourself small happen unconsciously, and they might not be obvious. They happen as you form beliefs about yourself from a very young age. Without even realising it you are replaying those beliefs and behaviours over and over again.

Find the belief, give it up and you will change your whole life.

My deep sensitivity to rejection among other things listed above, developed into beliefs that it was not safe to be seen or loved. You might recognise some of these not-so-obvious signs of low self-esteem, from different times in my life:

- Procrastination: Always putting off what I wanted to, or needed to do, especially if it was things that would be good for me to grow, or things to push my business forward.

- Analysis paralysis: Having a very hard time making decisions due to trust and belief in myself.

- Overwhelm: Having too many ideas or things to do and not knowing where to start.

- Extreme Busyness: Feeling constantly out of control, rushing around, too busy doing ALL the things to focus on what I really needed or wanted to do.

- Perfection: A desperate need to perfect everything and not get anything wrong, made it that everything took *so* much longer than it should, and honestly most projects did not even start as I was too frightened to get anything wrong to even begin.

- Burnout: A tendency to say yes to everything, and to do more than my share all of the time and an exaggerated sense of responsibility for the actions of others, which left me with no fuel left in my own tank.

- Extreme people pleasing.

- Avoiding close friendships and relationships, preferring to do things alone.

- Unhealthy close relationships with addicts.

If you are curious enough, try these processes that help you to see the not-so-obvious ways in which you hold yourself back:

- Start a meditation or yoga practice so your mind slows down and you can hear your inner voice speak to you.

- Look for things you *do* or *don't* like in other people, as everything in life is a mirror of you.

- Question what's going on wherever and whenever you get stuck on something.

Thoughts are not the truth: We are the ones that decide we are not good enough and therefore we also have the power to change this around

Creativity is a term used for artists and creatives, but creativity is not just for artists. We create our life with our thoughts, our beliefs, our choices and how we speak to ourselves. We also have the power and option to change all these things, create a new identity and express ourselves in a different way.

It starts with the knowledge that our thoughts and what we think or believe about ourselves are not the truth, and that these things can be changed.

The best way to start changing how you feel about yourself, loving, accepting and valuing yourself is in your subconscious mind using cognitive reprogramming. You do this in alpha or theta brain wave states, crowding out negative beliefs, thoughts and creating new neural pathways with things like 'I am' statements or positive affirmations, visualisations and belief clearing.

We allow ourselves to be loved, seen and heard at the speed of safety

We can only express ourselves, be loved, receive and be successful as much as our nervous systems will allow.

If you want to try something new or change how you are and it is not happening as fast as you would like, learning more, and doing more will not help you. The truth I discovered is a large part of you wants you to stay small, stuck in your patterns and your unique sabotage techniques.

Why? Your mind is addicted to being how you are or have been all your life, even if that is lonely, unhappy, unwell, stuck or small. It likes what is familiar and what is predictable. And it will only allow as much love, success and wealth as it feels comfortable with. Within familiarity there is comfort. Within a new experience (happiness, success, more money, self-love even), there are a lot of unknowns – and so this creates fear and resistance to the beautiful new thing.

To get past this, you need to constantly tell yourself you are safe to do more, by working on your nervous system and approaching things in small, gentle steps until you are ready to do more.

My favourite way to do this is Yin Yoga. A gentle movement that slows down your breath so you deeply relax and release trapped stresses and emotions.

Self-expression is not just for artists, and it is not just making art

In your personal life, your job or business, more knowledge, skills and processes make you smarter and more competent. Knowing who you are and what makes you different – and then learning it is safe to express that – *makes you powerful.*

Self-expression is not just for artists. Most people use self-expression every day to get their needs met and express how they are feeling. Our ability to do this comes from our self-esteem and level of self-compassion.

Common ways that people in your life might express themselves from positivepsychology.com include:

- Sharing details about their day and how it made them feel.

- Wearing an off-trend or outdated item of clothing, but just because they like it.

- Yelling to express their frustration about traffic.

- Employing body language that tells others how they feel about themselves – whether it's tall and proud, slumped and defeated, or anywhere in between.

Self-expression is also the key to unlocking and receiving EVERYTHING you desire and deserve out of life – *love, success, happiness, freedom, wealth, or whatever else it may be.* It's the very thing I now use to connect meaningfully with others all around the world and to have friends who prioritise and value me, instead of feeling desperately alone. To control my own life as opposed to being controlled by others; to reduce my anxiety and overwhelm; to ask for my needs to be heard and met and to set boundaries and protect myself. And there's so much more. Self-expression, allowed to finally be successful – to be seen and loved as someone of value and worth all over the world. Today I'm able to love and be loved, to be happy and to live a truly amazing life, totally my own way, outside of a 9-5 job.

Self-expression takes self-awareness, self-acceptance, and self-compassion *not art materials*; and it is the missing link to EVERYTHING I personally longed for almost 50 years, but did not have in my life.

SELF EXPRESSION EXERCISE:

Doodling, scribbling and free flow writing are excellent ways to encourage self-expression. Everything is exactly how it sounds. Grab a journal and start writing, doodling and scribbling. This exercise is not about perfection, creative writing or making a masterpiece. There are no wrong or right things to draw or write about, it is merely getting out whatever comes into your mind, without perfecting, questioning, analysing or planning it.

Being yourself is the most beautiful, valuable, and impactful thing you can be.

More often than not people search outside themselves for more success, happiness, and love, when actually loving, valuing and believing in ourselves creates the biggest impact. I personally spent most of my life madly trying to fix and change myself to be like everyone else as I believed that was how I would be loved. That is until I discovered the truth – *I am already love*. We all are. We simply need to believe this and be ourselves.

SELF-COMPASSION JOURNALING EXERCISE:

Your brain believes ANYTHING you tell it and it brings you evidence of anything you believe. These prompts are designed to change the way you feel about yourself and your life. I have MANY more. I usually write them in my journal and then cover them over with layers of different art materials. Please feel free to follow this link to 21 days of 15 minute, prompts and techniques you can use to learn to express yourself, value and love yourself more (with and without art materials) so you can start to shine out brightly and proudly, as you truly are.

What am I grateful for today? and/or What am I grateful for about myself today?

I am extraordinarily _____ insert whatever you want to bring into your life here. You don't have to be the thing you say you are already. Writing things you would like to be, creates new neural path-

> ways in your mind. Think: worthy, courageous, beautiful, loving, loved, lovable, creative, talented, successful etc.

And PS: Like Heidi Dellaire from *Love Wide Open* says here, always remember:

'You are beautiful
You are worthy
You are important
You are special
You are unique
You are talented and you are irreplaceable.'

References

- https://thriveworks.com/help-with/self-improvement/self-worth-vs-self-esteem/

- https://drjonicewebb.com/10-ways-you-may-have-been-emotionally-invalidated-as-a-child/

- https://uthealtheasttexas.com/news/finding-source-low-self-esteem-and-breaking-cycle#:~:text=Low%20self%2Desteem%20often%20begins,who%20were%20often%20very%20critical.

- https://www.betterhealth.vic.gov.au/health/healthyliving/self-esteem#causes-of-low-self-esteem

- https://www.psychologytoday.com/intl/blog/the-up-side-things/202011/what-are-the-roots-your-self-esteem?amp

Chapter Nineteen

Speak to Heal

Speak with clarity, certainty, confidence and impact and no matter what you do in your life ... speak for you.

> With Imogen Ingram, WomanSpeak™ leader and facilitator, delivering services to women in recovery from addiction and family and domestic violence, as well as circles for women in small business, middle management, and public facing roles.

The human story changes when women are the storytellers.

When women vulnerably share stories of healing and courage in the face of adversity, we become someone else's inspiration, and our lives emerge as a road map out of a place others don't want to be in.

When women lead with love, empathy, and compassion (as opposed to force and control) the resonance and frequency of our voices and presence have the potential to change the future of the world.

And yet, we forget that our humanity expressed through voice and body is where our power lies!

This is a story of learning to let my loving voice lead me, as I grew in understanding that my body's wisdom was with me all along. It's raw, predominantly joyous, and one I believe women need to hear. I hope it helps you to feel confident to share your voice again too.

Identity and women's voices

We talk a lot as women about the power of our voice.

Finding it. Using it. Trusting it. Losing it.

Individually and collectively.

While our experiences will be as varied as we are, I've discovered many, many women have had their confidence and identity derailed at some point in their life around using their voice. Living as a neurodiverse individual in a neurotypical world, burnout, losing a child, sexual or substance abuse, faith-deconstruction, social isolation, chronic illness, and perinatal depression come to mind.

Losing our voice is much more than the cessation of expressing ideas, opinions and perspectives vocally. Our identity, leadership, energy, and clarity of mind suffer. Often, the part of us that freely, playfully and creatively offers something to the world is irrevocably bruised or buried.

For me, losing my voice happened through a series of traumas over a five-year period.

When my Dad went missing after a bushwalk on the NSW South Coast in 2000, it was a brutal introduction to grief, fear, anger, confusion and paralysis. Legally declared dead, his body has never been found and our family's experience is a unique kind of mind-fuckery.

This happened while I was a pastor in a power-over, patriarchal, and driven church. A first-time mum, with no family support, who was suddenly also caring for a community as well as a newborn, I discovered that here in this church women's wisdom and feminine intelligence were silenced. This was embedded in the DNA of the international movement, spilling out with harsh reality. In addition, my husband came from a religious culture of a code of silence. Our cross-cultural experiences of parenting, leadership, and speaking up were very different.

I dropped into a gaping hole, lived in a permanent state of exhaustion due to insomnia and nightmares, financial stress, and constant dread. I repeatedly felt the sensation of a noose around my neck.

My husband and I eventually found the courage to leave this situation with our two beautiful toddlers in our arms. The day we left, we tangibly felt our own authority and self-determination return. It was like a switch had flipped. But what we didn't understand was the very real, ongoing impact of these traumas on my mind, body and soul. I now understand that my nervous system was highly dysregulated, and I was in a deep state of freeze. I literally felt locked away from experiencing emotion in my body and, for the first time in my life, in my early 30's, I was incapable of putting into words what was really happening inside for me.

Truth be told, I was in a darker place than I'd let on. Ironically, me, who – unlike my friends growing up – had never experimented with any substance, had gotten tangled up self-soothing with alcohol. Was I ashamed? Yes. Did I think it would pass? Yes. Did I stop drinking? Many a freeing time. But it never lasted, and I became self-isolating, angry, and silent; the impact on my family by the time I entered perimenopause was excruciating – for them and for me.

We don't need more restraint; we need to express and release

Until I asked for help – and used my voice to describe my living hell – the weight of my constrained emotions led to greater and greater suffering. I decided: No longer would I ignore the uncomfortable aspects of myself and carry on. To quote Leoni Waller (2024), *'I didn't need more restraint, I needed release'.*

Disrupting the cycle of drinking was impossible on my own. With gentle witnessing and co-regulation from others, my window of tolerance for the unknown (and the discomfort it brings) grew over time. Gradually, I didn't need to reach for something external. One of the most profound changes for me came through being seen and heard without judgement – not fixed, directed, or corrected – in circles with women.

Being with, expressing and alchemising feelings of discomfort – abandonment, doubt, shame, fear, confusion, anger, jealousy – is something very few of us are taught because we lack trauma-informed spaces and generational knowledge that normalise doing this. Fortunately, it's more okay than ever to speak about the wide spectrum of human experience. Phew!

As bushfires ravaged south-east Australia, and COVID altered the world forever, I was entering a phase of incredible clarity and inner propulsion. My process involved following my heart, re-training in circle facilitation, and joining a woman's speaking circle. I experienced a season of post-traumatic growth that opened extraordinary insight of purpose. By the end of the year, I left my 9-5 job and put myself first in a way I *know* my female lineage is proud of, and those yet to come will eternally benefit from. I will always thank my wise female boss at the time who encouraged me to put on my big girl pants and decide what was good for *me*.

You might be familiar with these three contexts, in which less restraint and more release are vital.

The first is perimenopause and menopause – that intense crucible of transformation, heightened sensation and emotional stripping bare! This season of life leaves many of us floundering and wondering if we *ever* knew ourselves! Self-doubt and the inner critic have an absolute field day! Erosion of a woman's true voice is a very natural consequence when this transition is handled clumsily, and without compassion or ritual.

Secondly, in working with female survivors of family and domestic violence, drug and alcohol addiction, sexual abuse, and those that have been in prison, I see the very real and effective protection mechanisms women have adopted because their lives – and their kids' lives – are in jeopardy. To stay safe, silence, appeasing, armouring up, and all kinds of complex survival strategies are required. 'Healing out loud because I nearly died in silence' (source unknown) takes on a whole new meaning in this context.

The third relates to honouring women's anger. David Bedrick (2024) describes anger as a form of intelligence, life force, energy, power, and clarity. Our families, communities, and the world need the release of our anger in safe spaces so we can offer this potent medicine for change with love.

Through all this, I have learnt that women *really* need each other to de-armour our hearts and unshackle our voices. For women, unlearning our voices as 'survival tools' and reclaiming them as true, powerful means for setting boundaries, conveying our rage, joy, vulnerabilities, and desires, while being witnessed by other women, is a journey of the most courageous kind.

A surprising healing modality for re-finding your voice and confidently sharing your story

Over the past five years, I have consistently made healing choices such as living alcohol free, using my voice, and intentionally cultivating love within and without. Among many impactful practices of being with discomfort, my greatest learning has come in offering women's public speaking training.

I also found that when women embrace and learn to harness the discomfort of public speaking, sharing their story can heal them, and begin to heal the world. Combine this with the genius of bringing a trauma-informed lens to public speaking and the training is super p-o-w-e-r-f-u-l.

How does it work? The discomfort you feel of being unable to speak up in front of others and use your voice with influence is not your fault and it is not a reflection upon you. It's a direct result of women and girls not having much of a choice beyond the 'stand and deliver' model of leadership and public speaking. The traditional masculine models taught in schools, in debating, and several organisations around the world are not designed for the feminine mind, nor for trauma to be felt and held safely.

Moving past all this is where the whole-life healing begins.

If a jolt of dread comes up weeks before professional development days, networking events, leading meetings, or giving a toast at a wedding, you're not alone. You know how it goes: Memorise your talk. Override your discomfort. Control your emotions. Grit your teeth. Get it over and done with.

Or if you freeze. Rooted to the spot. Sweating. Overwhelmed. Your words and voice literally evaporate. Somehow, it's over. What did you even say? Return to yourself – sort of. Afterwards, you're told *'you did great'* and *'it gets easier'*, but face aflame, all you want is for the floor to swallow you up so you can disappear!

You are certainly not alone. The great news is that there *is* a way forward, and within that process the deep healing begins.

Ancient wisdom, modern understanding, and a vital reframe

It begins with tending to our nervous system and paying attention to our bodies, before, during, and after we speak.

I one hundred percent know this to be true in my own body, and I have literally witnessed the rewiring of women's nervous systems through celebration in front of my eyes. It *never* gets old. Combine that with learning how to channel the energy that arises inside a woman's body, and you have something exquisite and extraordinary to work with.

The truth is, it can be deeply, excruciatingly painful to release our stories from where they are stored in our bodies, and to vocalise what we have experienced. Terrifying, traumatic, and unsafe are some of the words women have shared with me. We hold back on sharing our stories because we feel exposed. We keep them contained, tremulous that the darkness of our experiences will snuff out our light, and our well-worn pathways of pain will be dismissed, derided or used against us.

Finding connection with ourselves through connection with others

When emotional and psychological safety is established through voice and movement in circle, women are naturally able to engage with their deepest, truest expression. The process and time it takes for a woman to develop trust in her presence and use her voice with influence is uniquely her own. Speaking in front of others can become far more joyful when we understand and work with the truth that the *'fear of public speaking is the very real feeling of our power!'* (Kc Baker, founder of WomanSpeak™ and Velvet Flow, and a recognised expert on fear). Kc's reframe changed my mindset, and has empowered thousands of women around the world!

Over the years of facilitating feminine public speaking training, I've observed again and again the efficacy of combining ancient rhythms, practices, and profound reverence for feminine intelligence with real-life practical skill development. I adore hearing women's stories and thought leadership spoken with heart. In this refined feminine environment, there is vast invitation for presence, breath, pause and the wisdom of women's bodies to be celebrated full throttle. The resulting confidence and clarity empower women to say YES. Yes to presenting at medical conferences. Yes to speaking spontaneously at business events, and on camera, to offer exquisite eulogies, to have those difficult conversations, and even hold court at dinner parties.

I feel so proud to hold a space where performative pressure is replaced by deep listening, laughter, tears, and cellular level connection. Where women experience creative expansion of heart, body and voice – healing in community – in a way I've not experienced before.

And the oxytocin highs are like nothing else!

We *know* our world needs feminine leadership. No matter what you do in your life, speak for you! I am celebrating you as you speak with clarity, certainty, confidence and impact, and invite you to engage with feminine public speaking as a healing modality for your voice.

> **TRY THIS:** These are some of my favourite body-based practices to empower you to use your voice with confidence. I've made a video in which I guide you through a selection of exercises, including a simple EFT script, so you can connect with your energy, support your nervous system, and feel more at ease using your voice.

> **EXERCISE 1:** Practice these three effective ways women can increase presence and influence when speaking in front of others (this may be during public speaking, zoom presentations, important in-person conversations)
>
> 1. Plant your feet
>
> To ensure you feel secure, steady, and supported.
>
> Just as true if you are seated, speaking in Zoom meetings, or on social media.
>
> Done well, it does not mean becoming stuck or rooted to the spot.

2. Connect with *your* energy first

To stay connected with your power as you speak.

Practise a movement ritual before you speak – get tight energy unstuck.

Remember, the energy you're feeling is not all yours – it's coming at you from your listeners too!

3. Get in the room with your YESSS people

To practise receiving affirmation and celebration.

This is some of the most impactful nervous system work you can gift yourself for speaking impact (and life generally).

Be selective about your people – ask me how.

EXERCISE 2: Get playful to feel assertive – 5 things to try in your day

Hum what you see on your commute – feel the vibration in your throat and belly.

When it's your turn to speak in a meeting, lean forwards to insert your energy into the conversation, first using your body, then your voice.

Share a spontaneous 3-minute toast to *yourself* with a friend.

Shake it out for 30 seconds – really loosen your hips and limbs and say your name loudly three times from your deep, down belly space.

Connect with the base of your spine to open up your voice – take a 20 second walk, place your hands on your coccyx and breathe into the energy there. Notice how your chest opens up.

References

1. Baker, K. (2023) *Speak your truth. change the world*, *WomanSpeak*. Available at: https://womanspeak.com/ (Accessed: 07 October 2024).

2. Bedrick, D. (2024) *Why does anger so often get suppressed?* (Email accessed: 21 July 2024).

3. Waller, L. (2024) 'Emotions are wise and on our side', *The Undercurrent*, 11 August. Available at: https://leonawaller.substack.com/p/emotions-are-wise-and-on-our-side (Accessed: 08 August 2024).

Chapter Twenty

Sa Ta Na Ma: Powerless to Powerful

Re-finding your voice, during times of hardship and transition.

> With world renowned sound healing expert, and leader of White Swan Sound and Yoga Studio, Charlotte Fraser.

A clock that lost its tick,

A heart that lost its beat.

A drum that lost its rhythm,

A traveller that lost their way.

My heart was frost-bitten. Like many people who have been hurt before, I had placed my heart like an Inuit wrapped in animal skin and fur, inside a dark, spherical igloo with wizened light, far away from everyone. To truly meet me, it was a long, cold, freezy and almost unattainable destination. On the edge of the end.

I was a windmill on a still day. Simply not moving, unsure of what had happened, what was happening and what was to happen. Questioning purpose and composition.

Maybe you can relate when I say, *I was Frozen ... Stuck ... Waiting ...?*

LIFE as it was at the moment, if you could call it living

I distinctly remember the feeling of my seat bones on the hard floor in the chilly living room of my new rental as a recently separated and an almost 50-year-old mum of two young children, and deeply pondering my 'life situation'.

The creases of the synthetic white, but see through curtain hung still from the aged, yellowed plastic curtain rod. At the lowest point of the curtain a hand sewn hem almost touching the neither flat, nor brown, raised 70s carpet. Not a movement, not a breeze as I looked out through the curtains and noticed the blurred image of my outside world; like a still watercolour illustrated page in a children's picture book. Simply not moving.

Despite the disconnect, I observed how the outer world reflected my inner space. Like a broken windmill my body felt still and stuck. The memory of 'working' seemed long forgotten. A familiar, monotonous rhythm played in my head as regrets and memories rattled around in my skull like dense bones in a decomposed body secured in a redwood coffin travelling in a horse and buggy cart over an unsealed road. My heart felt like it had a pile of precariously balanced old, dusty books with once vibrant covers and gold leaf pages stacked inside it. Almost about to topple, just waiting to fall and tumble. Erratically balanced.

I knew it was time to open and read the 'books' which held the stored memories of my life so far, it was time to reflect, feel and restore. And so, the journey back to myself, started to unfold.

If you are in this with me, just know you are not alone. According to Healthline: *'By the time women reach middle age, it's likely that they will have experienced some trauma or loss. The death of a family member, a significant change in your identity, divorce, physical or emotional abuse, episodes of discrimination, loss of fertility, empty nest syndrome, and other experiences may have left you with a persistent sense of grief.'*

It makes sense that all these things lead to feelings of intense depression, anxiety, emptiness, unease, resentment and even remorse, and that these feelings get women questioning their entire lives.

DEATH of life as I knew it

It was at this time that my harmonium teacher shared with me the chant – Sa Ta Na Ma. Although I had heard and practiced many before this, this chant was particularly life changing at this time as it is helpful in times of transition. Sa Ta Na Ma means Birth. Life. Death. Transformation. The words of this chant come from the Sanskrit language; however, the words are actually ancient healing sounds combined to create words. So, you can focus on the meaning of the words, or the actual sounds, your intention. Chanting is the intentional repetition of a mantra, a mantra a release of the mind. The experience of chanting allows you to effortlessly drop into a meditative state. Most importantly it gets you out of your head and cracks your heart right open, allowing you to feel again. To feel all your feelings. To feel love and joy, to feel safe and peaceful, to feel stronger so your true voice can be uncovered.

Ever since I first heard chanting 20 years ago it cracked open my heart and drew me in, but at this time of transition, when my heart really needed healing, it was life changing. I was reminded over and over again how powerful chanting was to help me connect with my inner space, find deep content, joy and release old emotions. The rhythm of the repetitive words drew me into a very relaxed place where I felt like I had come home – to peace and to a place where I wanted for nothing.

At this time where everything was out of control and nothing was certain, it allowed my mind to focus, it interrupted all the chattering in my mind and gave me space and clarity, and it got me out of my woe-is-me victim mentality and focused my energy on moving forward. This allowed me to start removing the obstacles I had created in my life, to start to let go of all the garbage I had collected from 50 years of living, and *take back my life and my power.*

TRANSFORMATION: As we chant we see ourselves and life changing – giving space for a more authentic self to appear

As I chant, I hear my voice.

As I chant, I feel my heart.

As I chant, I share my feelings.

As I chant, I show my love.

And this allows for the expression of 'me'

And then I see the 'me' in 'you'

Chanting changed my whole experience of life. It gave me a space to hear my voice, and release emotions from my body that I was holding onto. Chanting works on a very subtle level but as I began to chant more, I became more connected with the feelings of my heart and live life on my own terms again.

In a world where I was socialised to be aware of what I said and how that may affect others, chanting was a chance to release sound from my body without feeling responsible for the effect it might have on others.

It's a place where I literally learnt to re-hear my own voice. The repetition helped me to become more comfortable with the sound of my voice and I started to feel more comfortable expressing myself according to my own needs. If I can do this, you can too. Your voice is an expression of your authentic self and style, and there is a great sense of freedom when you open and allow others to really see who you are.

Chanting helped me express, process and release my emotions – good, bad, happy and sad. Although far from perfect as a harmonium player or chanter, I was able to chant at my Mum's funeral, to process my grief through chanting and share her impact on my life.

Through my healing work chanting with others, I have seen endless evidence that it works for others too. Recently, one of my clients sent me an email to share her *'amazing and profound'* experience:

> *'When you sang Sa Ta Na Ma, I physically felt the grief and abandonment pain strong in my gut at the time, then it shifted. My heart opened and my headache eased and I felt calm and at peace afterwards. Then in the past 2 weeks I've felt an indescribable shift in being less frightened of death in general.'*

Chanting to other people gives me a chance to send love from my heart, and also an opportunity to express and care for others. As I began to share the bubbling and overwhelming love that sat in my heart, I found that this was echoed back to me through conversations with others after they had chanted with me. So, I began to share more love, and then I felt more love. This brings more joy to my life every day.

What about you? What would you like to change in your life right now? What would life be like if you were able to find your voice, express yourself again, open your heart and allow love?

Other life changing benefits of chanting for women in the midst of a transition

> 'Music is the most miraculous vehicle for opening the heart.'
> Ram Dass

Chanting works amazingly for many things, not just what I have already mentioned. I love these research-based positive health effects, and changes in the brain from withinhealth.com.

- Decreased negative mood

- Increased positive mood
- Improved focus
- Altruism and more compassion for others
- Boosted self-awareness
- A greater sense of calm
- Increased social connection when done in a group
- Reduced anxiety
- Better cognitive function
- Reduced fatigue
- Reduced blood pressure and heart rate in people with hypertension

How do I know if chanting is for me?

If you say yes, to one or more of these questions, then chanting is a brilliant way to heal and traverse the road to happiness, inner peace, self-discovery and of course self-acceptance.

- Do you often use 'I think' (as opposed to 'I feel') in conversation?
- Do you have big feelings and overwhelm?
- Do you spend a lot of time in your head?
- Are you coming to a new beginning in your life?

- Do you give your time to others and then find there is none left for you?

- Are you afraid to say what you really feel/think?

- Do you sometimes get stuck in a low mood?

- Do you feel disconnected from yourself and or others?

- Have you lost your way?

- Do you reserve love for just a few people in your life?

Birth. Life. Death. Transformation.

A clock that lost its tick,

A heart that lost its beat.

A drum that lost its rhythm,

A traveller that lost their way.

A clock that found her time,

A heart that found her measure.

A drum that found her song,

A woman who found her home.

Chanting literally saved my life at a time when I felt so down on myself – so close to broken, somewhat depressed and full of questions for myself. I have travelled this journey from being frozen, lifeless, afraid to hear my own voice to leading chanting at festivals in front of hundreds of people. I combine chanting wherever I can in my yoga classes, and every fortnight, as a part of a wellbeing program at a drug and alcohol rehab centre, where I share the joy and life-changing benefits of chanting with people in major transition.

You can chant and transform your life with me from anywhere in the world. I've recorded a version of Sa Ta Na Ma for you to use in times of change (that's a constant really!) so it's always helpful, but it is particularly helpful in times of significant change. Listen to Sa Ta Na Ma, say it in your head, whisper, chant or chant so loud. Practise it regularly and you will see the changes in your daily life! Notice the sounds of your voice, the feelings in your body, and the love in your heart and listen to what you need to or want to express.

EXERCISE: How do I get a chanting practice started?

There are many ways to chant, and many chants to choose from. To begin, start with Sa Ta Na Ma, as I have already made a recording of this for you. Follow the QR link to my recording.

You may want to choose something from nature (a beautiful flower, plant, crystal, ocean water) to keep nearby as you chant. This object from nature symbolises that chanting helps connect you with your own true nature.

When we chant, we are carving in a line in the sand from our daily life. So put a note on your door, find a quiet, warm and comfortable place to practise your chanting. Find a time and place where you know that you can chant without being concerned about bothering other people or being judged about your voice. Find a comfortable seat, feel your connection to the earth, with your spine straight and the front side of your body soft. It is always beautiful to start your day with some chanting as the sun rises.

Listen to the words of the chant and see them written down. Then close your eyes, start a couple of rounds of balloon breathing (deepen your breath and feel like there is a balloon expanding and contracting in your belly) and then start to chant. You may get the words 'wrong'; you may get the tune 'wrong'. Just allow this to happen as this is part of learning. You can start quietly and first, noticing the sounds, the rhythms and the feelings of the chant and its meaning. You may encounter some resistance with the repetition, and if so, keep moving through that until you feel like you have almost fallen into the sounds of the chant. Let your chanting be full of self nourishment – ask yourself – how does this chant need to flow to help me feel nourished? Allow yourself to move through the journey of the chant.

When you have finished, continue to keep your body still and let yourself notice the 'stillness' and the apparent silence. Take a few moments to notice and observe how it FEELS to be in your body. You may ask yourself – What am I feeling emotionally? How busy or quiet is my mind? How is my physical body feeling? How was this experience for me? What, if anything, has shifted or changed in me?

Allow your arms (the wings of your heart) to bring your hands to prayer at the heart. Feel your thumbs resting at your heart centre, reminding yourself of the love that sits within. Bow down to the effort you have made for yourself today and close the practice by thanking yourself for taking the time to get to know yourself a little bit more!

And remember, chanting is a practice, so the more you practise, the more you will notice the changes emerging in yourself and your life.

Research-based references for facts from withinhealth.com.

1. Perry, G., Polito, V., & Thompson, W. F. (n.d.). *Chanting meditation improves mood and social cohesion*. Retrieved April 11, 2023.

2. Gao, J., Leung, H. K., Wu, B. W., Skouras, S., & Sik, H. H. (2019). The neurophysiological correlates of religious chanting. *Scientific Reports*, *9*(1).

3. Moss, A. S., Wintering, N., Roggenkamp, H., Khalsa, D. S., Waldman, M. R., Monti, D., & Newberg, A. B. (2012). Effects of an 8-week meditation program on mood and anxiety in patients with Memory Loss. *The Journal of Alternative and Complementary Medicine*, *18*(1), 48–53.

4. Arora, J., & Dubey, N. (2018). Immediate benefits of "Om" chanting on blood pressure and pulse rate in uncomplicated moderate hypertensive subjects. *National Journal of Physiology, Pharmacy and Pharmacology*, *8*(8), 1162-1165.

Chapter Twenty-One

Miracles. Magnetism. Meaning.

The secret ingredient to getting everything you want and desire.

> With Lynn Hord: Breast cancer survivor, messaging specialist and business coach who supports hundreds of women globally to infuse heart, soul and meaning into their messaging, so they are seen, sought after and successful.

The year I turned 40 I felt so incredibly frustrated by life. I remember saying to my coach at the time: *'I feel like I've been doing all the 'the right' things. I've worked hard at being a good, kind human and followed all the 'rules' but my life isn't getting any better. I just don't understand.'*

Opportunities weren't showing up, my business wasn't growing and neither was my income. I felt lonely a lot of the time and my love life, well, it was a shambles. I just didn't get why other people's dreams were coming true but not mine? Have you ever asked yourself that too?

By this point, I'd been doing self-development work for 15 years, I'd been a trained life coach for 9 years and thought I was living by the spiritual

Law of Vibration, which says we can attract anything we want if we are a vibrational match for what we desire.

Honestly, after all the 'work' I'd done on myself, I thought my vibe was pretty high! But life was showing me I was clearly missing something – because I sure wasn't attracting what I wanted.

Then I was diagnosed with breast cancer just before I turned 42. And the year that followed taught me what I had been missing – that I wasn't being truly authentic in my life. Rather than live from my truth, I was living from fear. Rather than trusting in life to flow and support me, I was holding on to control for dear life.

Why am I talking to you about authenticity? Because it's THE HIGHEST frequency humans can emit (in fact it's 4 times higher than even love), which makes it one of the fastest ways to magnetise what you want.

Living authentically has changed my life – I am no longer that stuck woman who felt like everything she wanted in life stayed at arm's length. Instead, I feel like I know how life works. The more I have committed to living authentically, the more my life has filled with joy, love, connection, adventure, opportunities and money.

And I know it can work that way for you too. Below I'm sharing my story and the simple principles that will help you lean into authenticity so you can become naturally magnetic to YOUR heart's greatest desires.

Drop the masks to reveal the real you

When I was a kid I was badly bullied for years. And as a sensitive young thing, every mean word that was said to me was like a dart to my heart. I believed it all. My recess and lunch times were often filled with comments like: *'No one likes you Lynn, so get lost.' 'Stop bragging about being dux.' 'You're disgusting, go away.'*

I felt so much pain from the cut of other people's careless words that I made an internal vow to never hurt someone with mine – ever. Over time I learnt to either to just not say anything at all, or only say what other people wanted to hear.

I spent decades silencing my own voice, hiding my true thoughts and feelings, and playing down my achievements. And over that time, I suffered from depression, low self-esteem and severe loneliness (even though few people could see that from the outside).

It wasn't until my mid 30s I started putting two and two together – I craved authentic connection, but I was so afraid of being vulnerable and showing the real me that my inner barriers made that almost impossible.

Until my breast cancer diagnosis in August 2018.

My first 6 months of treatment was chemotherapy, which I've dubbed 'The Shedding'. Chemo left me with no energy to be who I normally was or to show up for others in the way I usually did. It was deeply confronting as it revealed to me all the behaviours, identities and false beliefs I had about who I thought I needed to be in the world in order to be loved.

I vividly remember about one month in, I sat on the couch talking to one of my best friends and I burst into tears and said, *'I'm afraid you're going to leave me because I'm not going to be able to give to you for awhile.'* She replied: *'I'm not going anywhere Lynn.'*

You see, I fundamentally believed that in order to get what I wanted – love, care, kindness, support – I needed to give first. I didn't believe that I was worthy of those things without 'earning' them. And the last thing I wanted was to be seen as 'needy'. But I was needy. I needed help, support, care, love and compassion like no other time in my life.

And, in contrast to some of my deepest fears, people didn't drop me because I couldn't be there for them, but instead stepped up where they could. They drove me to chemo, delivered meals to my door, took me on walks, let me cry on their shoulder, cleaned my bathroom, washed my sheets and so much more.

In the face of the flood of love, care and support I received, my inner walls crumbled. I had never been so vulnerable in my life, yet that opened the door to more connection, intimacy, tenderness and acceptance from friends and family than ever before. It was like the more real I was, the more people leaned in and showed up.

Most of us are conditioned as we grow up to be a certain way, ways that are acceptable and, we're told, will get us what we want. But these masks, if they're not true to our real nature, actually inhibit our ability to get what we want. So, you end up having to work SO hard to 'make things happen' because you're trying to do it through force of will, not attraction.

One of the deepest truths I learnt from cancer was this: that all of us are innately magnetic and life is so much easier when we're not trying to pretend we are anything other than who we are. If we have the courage to drop the masks and be vulnerable, it opens the doors to more freedom, connection, joy and success!

> **EXERCISE:** What's in the way of your natural magnetism?
>
> Gaining self-awareness around where we might be wearing masks and what those masks are is a great first step toward letting out your natural magnetism. Think about a place or person where you don't think you're really yourself and ask:
>
> 1. What stops me being the real me? (Consider your fears, needs, or expectations of you)
> 2. What would I do differently if I could?

The truth WILL set you free

Do you know in practice what authenticity really is? It's when what you say matches what you believe on the inside. If you say, '*That's a lovely dress*' but that's not what you really feel, then you're being inauthentic.

On a day-to-day basis, being authentic is about telling the truth about your thoughts and feelings. And I'm not going to pretend that's always easy, but I am going to wholeheartedly tell you it is 100% worth the effort.

Because NOT telling yourself the truth is what keeps you stuck, swirling and chronically wondering why life isn't showing up for you like I did. The 'truth' is actually like an energy bubble inside your body. When it is expressed, that energy flows. When we try to lock down that truth, it COSTS us energy to keep it hidden.

July 2019 was the 12-month mark for my breast cancer journey. I'd been through 6 months of chemo and a 10-hour surgery, followed by 2 months of recovery. And I'd been declared cancer free after my breast tissue had been tested for cancer cells and none were present!

The doctors still advised me to do a 15-day course of radiation treatment just in case. And I was totally onboard, until day 5. As I was laying on the metal slab, naked from the waist up, arms above my head, waiting for the machine to zap my right side chest, I suddenly started questioning why I was there.

Was this actually doing me more harm than good? Would it cause me problems in the long run I could have avoided? A wave of agitation hit me so hard I wanted to jump off the table. But I couldn't move or distract myself so I did the only thing I felt I could in that moment – I stopped trying to avoid my thoughts and feelings and faced them.

I admitted to myself that I was afraid I'd made the wrong decision. That I didn't want to be there on that metal slab. That I didn't want to die. And that I REALLY wanted to live a long life.

And Oh my God, the sweet release! Tears rolled down my cheeks, my body relaxed and my mind opened. The agitation melted away, I felt calm – and I could think clearly again.

This is the power of admitting the truth – it's energetically and emotionally liberating! And it is also the greatest skill you can master to clear the way to being radiantly magnetic so you can attract the love, joy, abundance and wealth you desire in this life.

Because when you admit your truth, you live with integrity, connect through vulnerability, and declare what you want. And to get what you want, you first have to admit the truth of what you think, how you feel and what you really want ;)

> **EXERCISE:** Think about a circumstance in your life right now that's causing you tension and write out answers to the four questions below. You'll feel that sweet release too when you're completely honest with yourself.
>
> What's the truth around this situation and:
>
> 1. What you think?
> 2. How you feel?
> 3. What you really want?
> 4. What you're afraid of?

Bravely follow your heart's desires

Surviving cancer wasn't the end of the story, it was just the beginning. It changed me fundamentally and awakened in me a desire to live from my genuine heart, not my head, speak my truth and create a life based around my heart's greatest desires.

I knew that to create that, I had to live by the principle's cancer had taught me – stop pretending, tell yourself the truth, and live with authenticity, integrity and courage. It took time to figure out exactly what that meant for me in reality. And even once I knew what changes I wanted to make, I resisted because ... I was afraid.

It would mean change, facing my fears, owning my gifts and brilliance and sharing my truth with the world. And that was both confronting and terrifying!

But the biggest thing that changed after facing death and surviving? My commitment to living a life I loved had grown so much stronger than the fears that used to stop me – particularly my fears around what other people would think, say or do if I said what was in my heart or pursued my greatest dreams.

In February 2020, a month after I got medically discharged, I could feel my heart's desire to be nearer to my family and experience the support and connection of having them a short drive away, not a 24-hour flight. So, I packed up my life in the UK and moved back to Australia after 9 years away.

Since then, slowly but surely, I made changes my heart was calling me to make.

I simplified my life and lived by the beach for two years, so I could be still, heal, rest and recover.

I overhauled my business so that it reflects who I have become and the kind of soul work that lights me up! (And I've almost doubled my income as a result.)

I have spent so much quality time with my family, and my heart has overflowed with connection, love and laughter.

I followed the desire to travel overseas for 3 months to the US and UK in 2023 and felt so alive again.

I loved the digital nomad lifestyle so much, I just kept living it even when I arrived back in Australia (and am still going a year later!).

A friend called me for my birthday in August 2023, while I was still travelling in the UK and she asked, *'How are you?'* And replied, *'I am really, really happy!'* Honestly, that answer took me by surprise. Because my life wasn't perfect or where I 'wanted' it to be – yet I was still HAPPY.

One of the final things the whole cancer business taught me was this – just how RICH I already am. In love, support, connection, joy, community, care, adventure, friendship, intimacy and courage. And when you think you're already rich and abundant, what does that do for you? It makes you even more magnetic to more of that.

EXERCISE: In order to bravely follow our heart's desires we need to know what they are. Imagine for a minute that you can have a proper conversation with your heart (just suspend reality for a second if that's a stretch for you).

Grab a journal or a piece of paper, and ask your heart:

1. What have you been trying to tell me?
2. What changes do I need to make?
3. What do you really want?

Uncover what you really want to share, so your content easily attracts soulmate clients, by following the QR link to my Heart Talk Guide.

Ask anything else that comes to you, and just let the words flow. Don't judge them or censor them, just stay curious to what comes to you.

If this kind of exercise is new to you, it's a wonderful practice to begin strengthening your connection to your inner voice, knowing and intuition. It might feel awkward at first, but keep going and with practice you will get so much better.

For far too much of my life I did not believe what I wanted mattered, that my truth had any power to create change, and that I could have a life that made me truly happy! Now, I am a successful writer, speaker, and spiritual entrepreneur. In over 11 years in business I have helped hundreds of women globally to infuse their heart and soul into the message they bring to the world and their purpose-driven work.

Conclusion

The whole human story changes when women are the story tellers.

We have lived in a world led by masculine voices and energy for thousands and thousands of years. A world driven by power, domination, anger and intolerance to the differences of others. More than ever the world needs to hear feminine voices and be led by the more feminine energies – love, empathy, nurturing, compassion, intuition, creativity, curiosity, collaboration, problem solving and kindness.

Our healing, our self-care, our self-study and our voice matters and we have the potential to change the entire future of the world ... yet our own stories, what we tell ourselves consciously and subconsciously, often hold us back and keep us quiet, unhappy with ourselves and small. We tell ourselves constantly that we are not good enough, not worthy enough, that we are not smart enough and that we don't know enough, when actually we ALL DO and we ALL ARE!

Every woman is smart enough, worthy enough and strong enough and has the power to live fully, to embrace joy, and to carry themselves with dignity, regardless of the difficulties they face. EVERY WOMAN! And this book demonstrates over and over again that it's true.

Every woman's biggest belief is, 'I am not enough'. Most people speak unkindly to themselves and do not like or value themselves enough (until they know better) and most of us experience a time or times of incredible hardship (especially in midlife), a dark night of the soul perhaps, where our sense of identity is shattered through big life change, loss, betrayal or tragedy. There is no doubt these times are very challenging, but they are all given to us so we can heal ourselves, forgive ourselves and love ourselves, become stronger and shine out as brightly as we can be.

In times of challenge please always remember, what I have experienced and truly believe … that despite all the (self-imposed) imperfect parts, the most beautiful thing we can all be is ourselves.

That giving ourselves compassion and love is the way we create the biggest impact in our lives and everyone around us.

That we don't need to fix or change ourselves. We instead need to understand the truth that we are already love, and simply need to love ourselves more.

That we don't just create art, music, dance etc. We are all creators who create our lives with our thoughts, beliefs and reactions to things. With this knowledge, we have the power to change anything about our lives.

That every woman has the ability, qualities and power to embrace love and joy and to live fully regardless of the difficulties they have faced, or are facing.

That we all have unique life experiences, special gifts and embody unique and essential qualities we can harness to not only transform our own lives – but to help heal the world.

That everything works better – our lives, our relationships, our careers, our businesses etc. – when we learn to be, accept, like and express ourselves.

That women's voices and women's energy naturally can impact and change the world.

And that REMEMBERING WHO YOU ARE makes the biggest difference in your life and everyone around you – not pleasing, controlling, changing yourself or fixing everything that is wrong with you.

Feeling good about yourself, your life and feeling up to taking on the world does not happen overnight and in fact your life probably will get worse on this journey before it gets better, as the universe pushes you to become the strongest, smartest and more resilient version of yourself. But, to start … all you need to do is take one baby step at a time.

Start today.

Choose something that you like the sound of and feels achievable from this book and begin.

Even if you can't be bothered, do it again tomorrow.

Once you incorporate that change, try something else new.

Repeat, repeat, repeat.

Sure, starting might be frightening, unknown and scary, and the journey certainly can be challenging, but the whole world desperately needs to hear from you to heal. To experience the love inside of you and everything you have to give and offer.

Your voice, your experiences and your story are sooo important, and these very things when shared connect you to others, where suddenly you find you have a huge life purpose and also that you are finally not alone.

My hope is that you find your voice, your joy, your longing and your power. That you connect deeply and lovingly with others. That you tend to your life, relationships and work with more love, ease, joy and gratitude through the stories, strategies and exercises shared in this book.

As L.R. Knost says here:

> *'Tell your story.*
> *Shout it. Write it.*
> *Whisper it if you have to.*
> *But tell it.*
> *Some won't understand it.*
> *Some will outright reject it.*
> *But many will*
> *thank you for it.*
> *And then the most*
> *magical thing will happen.*
> *One by one, voices will start*
> *whispering, 'Me, too.'*
> *And your tribe will gather.*
> *And you will never*
> *feel alone again.'*

Acknowledgements

I didn't plan to lead a book project, I was led to it by slowing down, listening in to my own inner intelligence and noticing all the little soul nudges and signs from the universe. I am sure glad and grateful I did, as I have met and collaborated with some of the most amazing writers, healers and thought leaders in the world, who I now consider my friends.

To all these writers, thank you so much for expanding my heart by sharing your life with me, and for vulnerably sharing your stories with the world. Your stories lead with love. They are filled with grace, warmth, poetry and insight and I am so impressed by how well they guide readers through your challenge-to-triumph style life stories and inspire others reading them to live the best life they can. It took a lot of courage, empathy, time and skill to do this and I am forever grateful that we now share this amazing book together.

To the incredibly amazing and talented Rose Mascaro from *HeartWriting* who jumped onboard to teach us all how to write from the heart using her very own *HeartWriting* processes, while also teaching us to use professional writing techniques. Thank you so much for your time, incredible knowledge and for sharing your generous, loving and enormous heart with us. You are AMAZING!

To my two beautiful art students that bravely believed in me and my vision and came along just for the ride, only to find out in the process that they are actually amazing writers with valuable things to share. Thank you for believing in me and for your enormous courage to try something way out of your comfort zone.

To my ever present and extremely caring and loving teen Mikey. Thank you for your support, friendship, patience with me and for giving me space when I am (quite often) on a creative wave of brilliance or hyper-fixation and cannot possibly get anything else done. You are my reason for being, for healing and for breaking old patterns. So I can love and support you in the way that you need, I have been making myself the most loving version of myself I can be. I am forever grateful for this and I love everything about you so much.

To Sarah Walkerden from The Rural Publishing Company. Thank you for your amazing support, knowledge and patience with the endless questions and demands I fired at you. I am forever grateful that you gave me chance to write and publish this book, with no prior experience, no writers signed up nor evidence that I could do this.

To Kia Miller and Kim McNaughton, you came onboard to not only write and share your story but to share something with us. Thank you for your incredible insight, generosity and the techniques you taught us around money and authentic community building, and how these things actually both relate back to inner work, how we feel about ourselves and how willing we are to be seen and to receive. WOW I was so blown away by the calibre of what you taught us. Totally lifechanging and I am so grateful for that.

ACKNOWLEDGEMENTS

To my beautiful, big hearted friend and contributing author Suzie Forbes who volunteered her time to set up and run a pre-launch book summit for us all. Thank you, I am incredibly grateful and would not have done this without you.

To you the reader, thank you so much for buying this book and for taking the time out of your busy life to read it and even more so, for taking the time to do something for yourself. Enjoy, thank you and I would love to connect with you more.

Thank you to my mother and siblings who always support me, and both my parents who encouraged me to follow my dreams and live life out the box, my own authentic way.

Finally to myself (since this book is about self-compassion, self-acceptance and self-love), thank you for your courage, creativity and for all of your knowledge. Thank you for saying yes to crazy ideas that most people would not dare to do. Thank you for your big heart, your deep sensitivity to everything and your empathy. The way you think more deeply and see things differently to others and for your ability to connect all sorts of random things and people together and make something magnificent. Thank for your care for the world and other people, the way you see beauty in everything and for being brave enough to vulnerably share yourself so openly with the world.

Don't let the stories stop here

If you are a creative, healer or thought leader who wants to learn more about how authentic self-expression and self-compassion magnetise everything you want and desire in life

If you want to share YOUR story, take part in a collaborative project, or run one yourself

If you would like to surround yourself with women who see you, support you, love you and lift you

If you want to impact or make your mark on the world

or If you would like to connect to extraordinary women that have (or are facing) their shadows and are successfully leading with love.

Click on this QR code and Join our Lead With Love community

Where we connect, share, support each other to shine out brightly, make impact and begin to change the world with our voices.

ADIE McDERMOTT
Authenticity is true beauty

Connect with Adie
adiemcdermott.com
adie@adiemcdermott.com
or @artbyadiemcdermott